Another
101
Best of
TUNNEYSIDE
of Sports Columns

Dr. Jim Tunney
"Dean of NFL Referees"

ISBN: 978-1-60679-350-3
Library of Congress Control Number: 2015960694
Book layout: Cheery Sugabo
Cover design: Cheery Sugabo
Front cover image: iStock/Thinkstock

Coaches Choice
P.O. Box 1828
Monterey, CA 93942
www.coacheschoice.com

Dedication

First and foremost is my gratitude to my wife, Linda, for the countless hours she allowed me to spend in my "man cave" each week while writing these articles. Her patience and understanding was beyond my wildest expectations. I love you!

Further, I dedicate these writings to my family and friends who read the many columns/blogs and have offered their wisdom and comments.

Acknowledgments

Words of gratitude pale in comparison for my true feelings of gratitude for John Oldach, an independent editing and writing professional, for his expertise in the edits and review of the content and context of these writings.

My appreciation as well goes to Dr. Jim Peterson and his great T*E*A*M at Coaches Choice for their wonderful collaborative efforts in making this book a reality.

Foreword

Growing up in Seaside, California, gave me a wonderful childhood and the opportunity to meet Jim Tunney (more on that acquaintance later). My father, Herman, Sr., was a Master Sergeant at the Fort Ord Army base, where I spent a lot of time with him. Most of my other time was devoted to playing sports. Wherever there was a game, I was in it. In my younger days, it was at the Boys Club (as it was called then). In high school and college, I mostly concentrated on football. After graduating from San Diego State, I was fortunate enough to be invited to play for the Philadelphia Eagles—invited, not drafted—where I played 10 years in the NFL.

Because that Boys Club was just a "shack," in my off-seasons with the Eagles I returned home and decided to raise funds to build a new and better club. That's when I met Jim Tunney. It was the early 1980s when Jim moved to the Monterey Peninsula and was working as an NFL referee. Player and official—we had a common interest in helping the youth in our community. I had organized a golf tournament to raise funds and asked Jim if he would be the master of ceremonies at our tournament dinner. He didn't even play golf, but gladly accepted my invitation. We conducted that tournament for some 10 years, and he was there every step of the way.

As we moved on from golf tournaments to football youth camps and other fundraising activities, Jim never hesitated to be of help in any way he could. He is very passionate about helping kids. In 1993, he founded the Jim Tunney Youth Foundation (JTYF), which "supports community programs and resources that work with youth to develop leadership, work skills, and self-esteem. The emphasis is on programs that work one-on-one with kids, not just to identify problems that hinder, but also to illuminate possibilities, and increase realistic options for building productive, self-determining lives." He invited me to be on the JTYF board of directors, which I have been for over 20 years. To date, the JTYF has made grants to local youth organizations in excess of a quarter of a million dollars.

To raise funds for the foundation, Jim created an event called SPORTSNIGHT, where he invites a prominent sports star to be the guest speaker. Over the years, Joe Montana, Ronnie Lott, Steve Young, Don Shula, Johnny Miller, Andrew Luck, and yours truly (among others) have stepped up to fill that guest speaker role. However, the uniqueness of these

SPORTSNIGHTs is the format. The JTYF sells tickets *only* to adults, who must buy a ticket for and bring a youngster (ages 8-18) to the event. The buffet dinner held in conjunction with the event features hamburgers, salad, sliced turkey, ice cream, sodas, and water—all donated. Everyone gets an autographed T-shirt and listens as these high-profile athletes tell stories that are designed to inspire both kids and adults.

These athletes donate their time and talent to help as a result of their connection with Jim, who was a 31-year NFL official, and who officiated four Super Bowls (two back-to-back) as a referee. He also refereed 10 NFC/AFC Championship games and 25 Monday Night Football (MNF) games, when MNF was *the* game of the week, as well as six Pro Bowls. That's why he has been called the "Dean of NFL Referees" and has been nominated for the (NFL) Pro Football Hall of Fame 10 times. The Hall has never inducted an onfield official. Hopefully, Jim will be the first!

What impresses me most about Dr. Tunney, who has a doctorate in education from the University of Southern California, is that he doesn't ever "retire"—he *refires!* He has moved from classroom teacher to coach to high school principal to district superintendent to professional speaker—all the while being an NFL game official—to private school headmaster to college board of trustees to author. This book, *Another 101 Best of TUNNEYSIDE of Sports Columns*, is the 11th book he has authored or co-authored. He continues to write a weekly newspaper column, currently in its 11th year for the *Monterey Herald*, called "On the TUNNEYSIDE of Sports."

Jim's book provides invaluable insights into the critical connection between sport and a values-based life. Whether you're a parent, an educator, or simply a sports fan, this book offers something for everyone. Enjoy!

—Herm Edwards

Herm Edwards played in the National Football League for 10 years. He then became an assistant NFL coach, then head coach of the New York Jets (2001-2006), then head coach of the Kansas City Chiefs (2006-2009). He currently serves as a football analyst for ESPN. He and his wife, Lia, and their two daughters continue to live on the Monterey Peninsula. Herm still conducts fundraising events for the Monterey Peninsula Boys and Girls Clubs.

Contents

Preface

It was my Speakers Roundtable colleagues at our 2005 meeting that provided the impetus for these TUNNEYSIDE articles/blogs. I have been writing a weekly newspaper column ever since. At first the column was to be called "On the TUNNEYSIDE of the Street"—a play on that old standard "On the Sunny Side of the Street," you know, "grab your coat, get your hat, leave your worries on the doorstep, life can be—" well, you get the picture. That title morphed into "On the TUNNEYSIDE of Sports." It is the belief here that sports issues—good/bad/right or wrong can prove to be positive examples for everyday living. The major emphasis of these articles is to take sports issues and transform them into positive messages to help others lead productive lives. I am confident that you will find a story in here that can make a difference in your personal and/or professional life. Now, it is up to you to make your life more fun, healthier, and more productive. Will you do it?

1 ATTITUDE

After further review …

There is no doubt that the U.S. of A. lost a true American hero recently with the death of Louis Silvie Zamperini at the age of 97. He was known as "Louie" throughout his life, beginning at school in Torrance, where he had arrived from New York with his Italian immigrant parents and three siblings.

Louie spoke little English and was bullied by his classmates until his father taught him to box. Fast-moving and pugnacious, he soon was whippin' everybody, and outrunning the cops on frequent occasions when they were in pursuit of the problem kid. Maybe that was the essence of being "unbroken" for him.

Louie's older brother, Pete, saved him from veering into a life of crime by introducing him to track. It didn't take Louie long to achieve success. At 17 he set a world interscholastic record in the mile, with a time of 4 minutes, 21.2 seconds. Then he won the California state mile championship at 4:21.8, which earned him a scholarship to the University of Southern California.

At 19, Louie qualified for the 1936 Olympics, being held in Berlin. With Adolf Hitler in the stands, Louie finished eighth in the 5,000-meter event (about 3.1 miles), running a remarkable final-lap time of 56 seconds.

Louie enlisted in the U.S. Army Air Force during World War II and became a commissioned second lieutenant in the Pacific theater. A bombardier on two of the infamous B-24 Liberator bombers, he survived intense combat in one and a ditching in the other. Louie and one other survivor spent 47 days at sea on a raft before landing in the Marshall Islands, and the remainder of the war in a succession of prisoner of war camps.

The details of his amazing experience can be found in Laura Hillenbrand's 2010 best-seller "Unbroken." The film of the same name, directed by Angelina Jolie, will be out this year.

We now turn to Lonnie Ballentine, 23, who had a great career playing football for the University of Memphis. Only great enough, however, for Ballentine to be drafted into the NFL by the Houston Texans in the seventh round, at selection No. 256—the final player taken. He now has the title of "Mr. Irrelevant." He was recognized last week at a banquet in his honor for his spot at the bottom of the draft. If perhaps he can find inspiration in Louie's life example and remain "unbroken," a full, honorable NFL career will be his.

 Will you maintain an attitude of never giving up?

July 28, 2014

After further review …

Many people resist change and would rather stay in their comfort zone—that's the "zone" where it's the same old, same old, and dependably unchallenging. Some proclaim, "Well, we've been doing it this way for a long time now and it has worked OK for us." The TUNNEYSIDE says poppycock! Speaking to corporate, business and education audiences, I encourage them to embrace change. It is an absolute truth that if you want to grow and get better at what you do, you must change. All growth requires change.

Being part of the National Football League for more than a half-century, I have witnessed many changes. Not only the size and speed of players, but coaching styles and types of play have changed dramatically. Yes, there are still 11 on each side of the ball and yes, it's still a physical contact sport. However, when the instant replay system was instituted in 1986 (this season will be its 28th), many resisted. In fact, the system was proposed some eight years earlier but was rejected. And when it began, it was on a one-year trial basis. It's there now for keeps.

Changing a culture takes time and commitment. The NFL officiating department may arrive at some changes slowly, but the commitment to excellence is there. As a contributing member of that department for this 2014 season, I am witnessing a positive attitude from the part of its 121 on-field officials. The NFL hires only the best college officials, but then begins to train each one to do the tasks before them better. Thus the expression: "Making the best better." When fans watch their favorite T*E*A*M, they expect only the best; and that's what the officials want—to be the best third team on the field!

NFL officials are well-versed in the philosophy of excellence, but there is also a physical aspect to officiating. Lightning Fast is a conditioning program that requires officials to be in top physical shape in order to keep up with today's players. That's not to say that officials were not in-shape before, but Lighting Fast emphasizes flexibility and movement that puts the official in the correct position for every play.

The protection of players is more important than ever before, with a greater responsibility placed on officials. Rules have been changed to ensure that everything is being done to provide the best game possible in today's environment.

 Will you embrace change with an attitude of getting better at what you do?

After further review …

As a behavioral psychologist and inspirational speaker, Dr. Eden Ryl's favorite topic was "You Pack Your Own Chute." Her emphasis was the idea that your behavior is created by you and that you should avoid blaming others for determining who you are. She disdained the expression, "Well, that's just the way I am," often used by people in a self-disparaging manner to explain away bad choices and behavior.

"Everyone is afraid of something" claimed Ryl, who admitted that the fear of skydiving was her nemesis. Determined to walk-her-talk, she parachuted from an airplane—more than 40 years ago. It was not a simple task then, but Ryl believed that you can "stretch yourself beyond self-imposed limitations."

Further exploring the maxim of packing your own chute, I recently met with Joe McBride, the executive vice president of digital marketing for StudioPMG, a company that creates and develops innovative digital marketing campaigns. McBride has never met Ryl, but certainly thinks along the same lines. He has completed over 1,300 successful jumps—as in departing from a perfectly functioning plane to fall through the air until the ground is met.

But curiosity about how to overcome the fear of free-falling from an airplane or base-jumping from the top of a massive cliff (think Grand Canyon) or structure, or skiing down nearly vertical Himalayan slopes meshes with the topic of packing your own chute.

McBride tells me that he overcame such fears through focus. Focus? Absolutely! Focus on your preparation, not the end-result. Fear, they say, is "false expectation appearing real."

Preparation is the hub of your readiness. With your thoughts centered on the details vital to your success, you'll achieve a familiarity with them that won't let you down when the critical moment arrives. Packing the chute, correctly positioning the body and knowing what to do while falling through space at about 120 mph are rehearsed to perfection before any attempt is made. Expert instruction must precede all of the details, so you can make a second jump!

Most all of life's events are based on one's preparation. Los Angeles Rams Hall of Famer Merlin Olsen often said, "The will to prepare is more important than the will to win." Landing safely from a parachute jump depends on preparation!

 Will you take responsibility for "packing your own chute" in everything you do?

February 1, 2015

After further review …

With the football season now behind us and basketball and hockey in full swing, we turn our attention toward Major League Baseball as players head to spring training. Surely, every one of them anticipates a successful season enough to embellish the memory of Ernie Banks. Banks, who died recently at age 83, was the epitome of enthusiasm.

"It's a beautiful day, let's play two," his signature phrase, expressed Banks' love of playing the game of baseball. Have we lost that in the professional game of baseball today? Surely our high school and college players—as well as those who love and play softball—would play two (or more!) whenever they get the chance. Banks would be proud of the legacy he created, but his was not an easy road.

He got his start with the Kansas City Monarchs of the Negro Leagues, and when he joined the Chicago Cubs in 1953, endured the same "You're not welcome here!" refrain that met Jackie Robinson when he joined the Brooklyn Dodgers.

Ernie's "… let's play two" was regularly followed with "… but not without you." Ernie's love of his fellow man and his team approach lifted the Cubs throughout the nearly two decades he played for them. The free agency that Curt Flood helped establish came years later, but even if it had existed, "Mr. Cub" never wanted to be anywhere except Chicago.

It's startling to consider that a first-ballot inductee into the MLB Hall of Fame in 1977 (512 home runs, .274 batting average and 2,583 hits) never played in a postseason, never had a sniff of the World Series. But Banks stood for everything right in the game, and I have always admired his character. It was my honor as an NFL official during the 1960s to work on that same Wrigley Field (at Addison & Clark) where he played. Then, on Sept. 15, 1968, I was privileged to referee the 100th NFL game between the Green Bay Packers and the Chicago Bears (Packers 28, Bears 27) at Wrigley. Wonderful memories there.

Many of today's MLB players have the same love for this game that Mr. Cub had. The baseball fans of today need to see and hear more about those who follow the Banks Creed.

 Will you look to Ernie Banks' legacy as a path for what you do?

After further review …

Robert Burns, Scotland's favorite son (unless you are Craig Ferguson fan), is regarded as the national poet of Scotland who wrote "Auld Lang Syne," often sung at Hogmanay—the last day of the year. A pastor friend of mine referred to that poem in a recent homily admonishing his congregation to not let it become ordinary. He was referring to those in his church who allow church to become ordinary, overlooking those who spend tireless hours preparing, planning and fundraising.

As we begin 2015, this writer is grateful to each of you who read these columns. The goal is to not allow any column to be ordinary. Further, the challenge is to not let events in one's life become ordinary, but treat each as a privileged opportunity.

Jan. 1 is a day of football for many. The NCAA decided to not let its bowl games become ordinary. For the first time they created a Division I Football Bowl Subdivision playoff. The Rose Bowl half of this playoff was won by Oregon, especially important to me since my daughter, Maureen, and grandson, Jake, are alums; but also because I grew up just four miles from the Rose Bowl—it's like a second home to me.

My dad was a football official and I attended many games (carrying his gear bag) in that "Granddaddy of them all." Sitting on the home team bench one game, my dad said, "Now watch this halfback (playing for Pasadena Junior College)—he is really something special." I was 9—sitting next to Jackie Robinson.

Later attending Occidental College, I was fortunate to play for the Tigers in the Rose Bowl. Further, I refereed many high school championships there, as well as the Junior Rose Bowl game (the national junior college championship) three times. When the NFL decided to hold Super Bowl XI (1977) there, I was fortunate to be selected as the referee. That game was 30 years to the month after my dad had refereed the 1947 Rose Bowl game. That stadium will never be ordinary to me.

 Will you treat every life experience in 2015 as more than just ordinary?

December 7, 2014

After further review …

It's time to draw the line on "unnecessary roughness" at game sites as well as in communities around our country. Football rule makers work diligently to create adjustments in order to decrease unnecessary and violent (helmet-to-helmet) hits on the field, stepping off penalty yardage and increasing associated fines. This includes college and high school games.

Drawing stricter lines also needs to apply to fans who declare their "hatred" of opposing fans through the use of violent acts. It's a game, not a war. Fights among spectators have become common, not only in the stands, but also in the vast and largely unsupervised parking lots, where shootings occur too frequently. What goes into the thinking of a fan who brings a gun to a football game?

Football is a physical sport. To call it a contact sport falls short; it's a collision sport. "Ya gotta knock somebody down!" is a coaching maxim. Blocking and tackling are integral to the game and that's what fans want to see. No one likes to see a player injured, although there are odious examples of fans cheering when an opponent gets carried off the field. Hey, that could be your son being carted off by the medics. What say you then?

This subject is not new to the sport or to the scrutiny of TUNNEYSIDE columns. Has the clashing of helmets in TV promos incited this? Does the repeated viewing of violent hits encourage fans to mimic? Having been up close and personal in witnessing such hits, I can attest to the damage they do, not only in the short term, but also later in life.

Recently more violence has found its way into communities in protest of disputed actions. Is the answer more security? Responsible entities have increased security for athletic contests. Is that the answer? When issues of domestic violence and/or sexual assaults occur in the sports world, education programs often figure in the outcomes. Can we, and should we, insist on programs for those involved in "unnecessary roughness" on our streets and in our communities? Violence begets violence. If a society can't insist on civility, it should find ways to instill it. It's the far better verb.

 Will you maintain an attitude of civility in your behavior on and off the field?

March 1, 2015

After further review …

The age-old question of how you measure potential in an individual or T*E*A*M will always be in the minds of employers. Gauging the value of a candidate's unknown future performance will never be simple. Let's direct our attention to one of that world's most talked-about sports evaluations—the Combine.

The NFL recently completed its annual "Combine," during which data on potential players was accumulated. Background on each potential draftee's medical history, psychological profile, functional movement, 40-yard dash time, and a "Wonderlic" score was gathered. This data was then poured over and over to the point, perhaps, of paralysis by analysis.

A Wonderlic? What's that? Developed some 80 years ago by Eldon F. Wonderlic (but constantly updated to reflect changing standards and mores), it's a test used to assess an individual's aptitude for reasoning and problem solving. The test consists of 50 multiple-choice questions to be answered in 12 minutes. A score of 20 would indicate average intelligence, corresponding to an intelligence quotient (I.Q.) of 100. Should we refer to it as "Wonderlic" or "Wonder-luck"?

The history and achievements of a candidate are studied. Is his college ability comparable to what he will be facing in the NFL? Can he give or take a "hard hit"? What is his potential for injury and/or recovery time? Those responsible for this collection of data, its analysis and application, must turn the numbers into usable assumptions in order to make a decision on the effectiveness of the candidate. How do we measure the heart of an athlete? Does that really count?

Not long ago I collaborated with former NFL Head Coach and now ESPN analyst Herm Edwards on a book titled "It's the Will, Not the Skill." Its purpose was to outline principles and philosophies of success, centering on Herm's advocacy of the will as the strongest tool in the pursuit of personal goals. His winning aphorisms are plentiful, but the one that speaks most simply and directly is this: "There's no 'quit' in my dictionary." He is well-echoed by Dick Adler and Jerry Ross in their song "You've Gotta Have Heart" from the musical "Damn Yankees."

 Will you include heart in your criteria in evaluating the potential of others?

December 22, 2014

After further review …

The film "Unbroken" opens on movie screens worldwide this week. Its story depicts the life of Olympic distance runner Louie Zamperini and how he overcame indescribable odds to survive World War II.

An Army Air Corps bombardier on a B-24 Liberator aircraft, Zamperini and his crew were conducting an aerial search at sea when the notoriously unstable bomber developed mechanical problems and crashed. Zamperini and two others were the only survivors. The trio drifted in a small raft for weeks, surviving on fish, birds and rainwater. One of the three died after a month; Zamperini and the other one survived but were captured by a Japanese patrol 47 days and some 2,000 miles from the crash site.

Thus began Zamperini's struggle as a prisoner of war, singled out for inhumane treatment and propaganda purposes by virtue of his Olympic fame. The title of Laura Hillenbrand's biography could have easily have been "Desire," considering how much of that quality Zamperini had to possess in order to live.

This story illustrates Zamperini's never-give-up attitude; that's where the word desire (to live) comes in. While this story is unique in its description, it was all-too-often repeated in WWII and in wars/conflicts throughout our history.

The lesson is to remind us that we must never forget what so many have endured to preserve our freedoms, and to remind us that we all possess an inner strength when faced with life-threatening situations. Whether it's a debilitating illness, an accident or a disabling family dysfunction, we need to maintain the desire to move life in a positive direction.

As in sports there comes a time when we face an opponent that we must struggle to overcome, and thus continue to fight to win and/or survive. It was sports that gave Zamperini that desire. The question remains: how does one know if he or she does possess such an inner strength? It's called belief, a word often employed by today's sports teams. It starts with "one small step," as astronaut Neil Armstrong taught us some 45 years ago. His desire to achieve was not much different than Zamperini's.

My heartfelt thanks go to each of you who have read these columns/blogs over the past 10 years. We wish you a peaceful holiday season and a merry Christmas.

 Will you adopt Louie's never-give-up attitude?

After further review …

As a cultural phenomenon, self-esteem is widely perceived to have gotten a running start in Western societies around the time that California Assemblyman John Vasconcellos created his "Task Force on Self-Esteem" some three decades ago. Actually we can travel back as far as William James and his "Will to Believe" published in the late 1890s, to observe the reach of this concept. It clearly has played a long and significant role in our sense of accomplishment and fulfillment.

Vasconcellos, who died in May 2014, believed that low self-esteem was the root of crime, drug addiction and other problems associated with the growth of young people. While there is no factual basis that his belief was the case, the TUNNEYSIDE supports youth organizations designed to develop self-worth in young people.

Can sports and youth clubs really help develop that highly sought-after characteristic? The belief here is that the opportunity to develop one's own values is enhanced when youths are surrounded by positive-thinking people. But the belief in oneself must come from within; outside help is ancillary to that process.

A recent HBO Real Sports program, hosted by Bryant Gumbel, focused on the widespread practice of rewarding trophies to everyone on the team, win or lose. In today's junior league sports, teams and leagues organized by parents are handing out trophies to players whose strikeouts and errors far outnumber their gems on the field; they're being rewarded for the "excellence" of simply showing up! Parents reason thusly: "We don't want to damage a player's self-esteem."

Now hold on just a minute. Lifelong experiences teach us the real world doesn't work that way. There is nothing wrong with losing! Life is a "trial and error" endeavor. Losing is not "failing" (that word sounds too final); losing is a setback, not an ending. If a player doesn't earn a trophy given to others whose will and excellence were better that day, it's not "crushing a dream." Further experience and helpful guidance are called for, and can help make up the shortfall.

Building self-confidence, and thus self-esteem, involves convincing an individual that losing and setbacks are part of the growth process. Sure, one has the right to feel disappointment; but it shouldn't be equated with discouragement. Trying again needs to follow disappointment; that's where improvement can be found. In any game, as in real-life situations, losing can strengthen one's resolve. It's called resilience!

 Will you maintain the will to believe in yourself?

2 CHARACTER

iStock/Thinkstock

After further review …

At first glance, this headline might prompt you to think it refers to how your T*E*A*M fared in formation of the NCAA basketball brackets. Or that perhaps, having just celebrated St. Patrick's Day, your lucky shamrock is trying to tell you something. Not so.

The "Luck" invoked here had to do with being in the audience at the Jim Tunney Youth Foundation Sports night dinner at the Hyatt Regency in Monterey. Some 400 youths (7 years and up) along with a group of host attendees (40/50/60 years and up) listened with rapt attention to guest celebrity Andrew Luck. He is now approaching his third year as the starting quarterback on the AFC South Champion Indianapolis Colts, having replaced the iconic Peyton Manning.

Andrew Luck was born in Washington D.C., but spent his early years in London and Frankfurt since his father, Oliver, was the general manager of the World League of American football. An unusual circumstance for an American kid wanting to play American football, but Luck made the most of it.

Returning to Houston, (where Oliver was the CEO of the Houston Sports Authority), Andrew Luck set many football passing records at Stafford High School, along with being valedictorian of his senior class. After considering several prestigious higher education offers, Andrew chose to attend Stanford University where he graduated with a degree in architectural design.

He was eligible to enter the NFL draft following his junior year, and projected to be a first round selection, but the lure of early departure was outweighed by his desire to finish his education.

In his engaging remarks to all the young faces in that crowd, Luck de-emphasized football glory and described instead how vital an education was. He said that for him, knowing the average length of an NFL player's career was less than four years meant he had to give serious consideration to "what I was going to do for my next 60 or 70 years after football was over." Reading, studying, and preparation were essential in his life, he said. That message hit home.

Some 800 eyes stared unblinking at this six-foot, four-inch Texan who was more like a big brother than a sports star. When someone asked about a memorable moment in his life, Luck smiled and recalled his younger brother Addison's success in a recent soccer match. That's a true role model talking.

 Will you pay attention to this Luck-y lesson in your own life?

January 27, 2014

After further review …

People often ask where the ideas and topics come from for these TUNNEYSIDE of Sports columns\blogs. The answer is simply by watching and reading about sports (and sports figures) of all types with an eye toward how a sports issue can help others. The TUNNEYSIDE belief is that sports can be a metaphor for doing the right thing, helping others, being responsible, and a whole list of desirable character traits.

The following item popped up just recently and has been widely seen and read about. A football player was quoted as saying, "Don't judge a person's character by what they do between the lines." Huh! Excuse me, but since the only behavior of yours that fans do observe is entirely "between the lines." That's when their judgment of you takes place. It's the only way a young athlete who looks up to you and wants to emulate his "hero" (I never liked that term) can judge you, your skills, or your character.

Superstars have a unique advantage in demonstrating to others proper behavior, respect for others and the game with the recognition of opportunities to "do the right thing." There are many in the business of professional worlds, e.g., doctors, lawyers, business people, etc. whose character would be admired and emulated if their profiles were more public.

It's a whole different premise with successful athletes; their acclaim, and the attention paid to it, is built right into the job. Like it or not, their public recognition puts them in a leadership position, so there should be the goal of doing the right thing—every time!

 Does your character exhibit a respect for those you live, work and play with?

After further review …

Incognito is an Italian word absorbed in English usage as an adjective or adverb that means "with one's identity concealed." However, a different sense of the word has lately emerged as relationship among teammates has become less concealed. A veteran player has been suspended by the organization for allegedly bullying a younger player. And so "Incognito" became a verb, and one that will persist if more instances of this sort of egregious behavior come to light.

Teasing, kidding and other forms of such behavior have been around a long time. But this behavior became so way out of line that it shut down the one intimidated. Each of us has boundaries to protect our dignity and honor. Yet, it is the intimidator who has no boundaries and thus violates another with acts of violence—verbal and non-verbal. The public was made more aware of violent behavior in the cases of sexual abuse of children and young adults.

Such harassment has become more widespread with the advent of social media, giving rise to a new term in the modern lexicon: cyber bullying. It signifies using the Internet to distribute untrue, inflammatory, and demeaning information about someone. A common trait of bullies is their contempt for the boundaries of personal dignity. Such bullying has driven many victims to the point of suicide. It doesn't have to happen.

"Harmony At Home" is a non-profit organization well described by its own name. Its mission is "to end cycles of violence and abuse by empowering children and young adults with knowledge, skills and confidence to lead healthy lives."

Harassment and the abuse of others have no place in a civilized society. Never be afraid to cry out: I need help!

Will you demonstrate the character to give or get help as needed?

May 4, 2014

After further review …

On occasion, my mom would call out from her kitchen, "Jimmie, will you set the table for dinner using our sterling silver flatware while I jump in my baby blue Mercedes and run to the store?" Her lighthearted reference to the silver and the Mercedes always came with a chuckle. We had neither. The NBA is without its "Sterling" forever, and good riddance.

NBA Commissioner Adam Silver has banned Los Angeles Clippers owner Donald T. Sterling for life from attending or being involved with the operation of his or any other NBA team. Three months at the NBA helm, Silver took an unprecedented action against one of the league's longest tenured owners in response to the release of a recorded conversation between Sterling and a young woman with whom he had a relationship. Sterling's contribution to the conversation was a finger-wagging, racist admonition that she steer clear of Clippers games while in the company of African-Americans such as NBA legend Magic Johnson. That kind of attitude from a man in his position is hard to fathom. I believe Silver made the right call.

Even before Sterling's identity was confirmed the report went viral, and his true characteristics were on display for all the world to see and hear. For many, it was not a revelation. Sterling bought the Clippers and moved them from San Diego to Los Angeles in the early 1980s. He attempted to hire former Villanova basketball coach Rollie Massimino to pull the struggling Clippers out of their dysfunctional state. Massimino said he terminated the interview when Sterling used racist terms to describe his players. The plantation-owner demeanor of Sterling is well documented, both in anecdotes and lawsuits. The latest episode is simply the most public one.

There was some talk the Clippers players would walk away from the playoffs. Silver's quick action removed that concern. But even without the commissioner's swift action, I think the team should have continued in its quest for the title. The integrity of the game counts most. And fans come to see players and coaches, not real-estate moguls.

There has been an occasional suggestion that Sterling's "advanced age"—80—was the real culprit, that somehow a bigoted display is excused in an "old white guy." Such a suggestion amounts to an apology for behavior that has no place in the evaluation of human beings.

 Will you show the consistency of your character in both private and public?

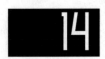

After further review …

With the NHL and NB seasons drawing to a close (whew!), the NFL has leaped back onto the media stage with its annual player draft. The final player selected—this year it was No. 256—is appropriately named "Mr. Irrelevant." I mean, what could be more irrelevant than a player chosen last? The regular-season NFL player roster numbers 53 players. Most NFL teams invite more than 100 players to training camp, including all those already on the roster. It is estimated that fewer than 100 newly drafted players will remain on the 32 teams. Then, too, the average tenure of an NFL player is 3 1/2 years. What chance does No. 256 have?

But I get ahead of myself. In 1975 Paul Salata, of Newport Beach, approached me and said, "I want to do something for someone for no good reason."

"Sounds like a good idea," I responded. "What's your plan?"

"Well, Salata continued, I want to honor the last NFL draft choice each year and call him 'Mr. Irrelevant.'"

Salata, called "Slats" by his friends, had played in the NFL as a receiver for the Baltimore Colts and the 49ers, following a stellar career at USC that included two Rose Bowl games. Tapping his own financial resources to fund this project, he created the event that is much the same today as it was in 1975. Each year, Mr. Irrelevant is flown to Newport Beach and honored with a week of celebrations.

When Mr. Irrelevant arrives in Newport Beach he is paraded by land and sea, stays at a luxurious hotel, then treated to a day in his honor at Disneyland, a golf tournament, and a featured horse race named "Mr. Irrelevant." The "Irrelevant" festivities conclude with a gala banquet, where he is presented with the "Lowsman" trophy. I've been a speaker at that event, which is always full of current and former NFL players and coaches, many of whom are Hall of Famers as well as a contingent of local celebrities. Only "Slats" could pull this off.

This year's Mr. Irrelevant is Lonnie Ballentine, a 6-foot-3, 220-pound safety from the University of Memphis. He was drafted by the Houston Texans and will be honored on July 10. It may well be the highlight (or lowlight) of his career.

 Will you think of something you can do for someone "for no good reason?"

After further review …

Well, if "sport" implies overcoming rigorous mental and physical challenges to achieve victory, then those who successfully complete the course do, indeed, meet the criteria. If the lessons of sport can inspire discipline and integrity elsewhere in life, then in the Navy SEALs we find yet another match.

Admiral William H. McRaven, an alumnus of the University of Texas and its Naval Reserve Officers Training Corps, earned a master's degree from the Naval Postgraduate School and went onto a distinguished career as a SEAL team commander and director of U.S. Joint Special Operations (including the mission that disposed of Osama bin Laden). McRaven delivered the Longhorn commencement address on May 17, drawing extensively from his SEAL experience, telling the assembled candidates "If you think it's hard to change the lives of 10 people—just 10—change their lives forever, you're wrong."

McRaven gave this example: "A young Army officer makes a decision to go left instead of right down a road in Baghdad and the 10 soldiers with him are saved from a close-in ambush." "Moreover," he said, "generations upon generations were saved by one decision, one person."

In McRaven's ethos the following simple points loom large:

Make your bed every morning. Admittedly it's mundane, but by doing so you will accomplish a simple task, which will encourage you to do another and another. Should your day turn out miserably, you'll at least come home to a bed that is made.

Find someone to help you paddle. Lives depend on SEALs paddling efficiently together, not singly. Neither can changing the world be done alone. Get someone to help you.

Life can be difficult. Failure is a certainty—and it may happen often. But if you keep working at the task at hand, success is possible.

Stand your ground. Navy SEALs are taught to survive encounters in shark-infested waters by exhibiting no fear and using a 'punch in the snout' if necessary. "There are lots of 'sharks' in the world, but if you want to change the world," said McRaven, "don't back down from the sharks."

The TUNNEYSIDE sees strong parallels between the character building in sports and Navy SEAL training.

 Will you give it your best shot using McRaven's advice?

After further review …

"Swimming is a major part of my life. But right now I need to focus on me as an individual," said Michael Phelps, unquestionably the most decorated Olympian of all time. He has won 22 Olympic medals: 18 golds, two silvers and two bronzes. Mark Spitz (nine golds) and Matt Bondi (eight golds) follow in gold medal count. But let's not omit Jenny Thompson, Dana Torres and Natalie Coughlin—each of whom has 12 medals.

Phelps' statement has little to do with his swimming prowess, but more with his appalling behind-the-wheel judgment. Phelps was arrested earlier this month for his second DUI which showed a blood-alcohol content of .14—twice the legal limit allowed by the state of Maryland. His arrest report indicated "excessive speeding and crossing double-line lanes in Baltimore at 1:40 a.m.!" "Nothing good happens after midnight," former NFL head coach Herm Edwards regularly reminded his players. Unfortunately for Phelps, he never learned the Edwards' Code!

USA Swimming, the governing body, suspended Phelps for six months. Good-on-you! Further, that same body banned him from next year's U.S. Team at the World Championships, as well as suspended his monthly stipend ($1,750). "I'll make a million mistakes in my life, but as long as I never make the same mistake again, then I'll be able to learn and grow," said Phelps. Good-on-you, Mr. Phelps!

Unfortunately, Phelps said that in 2012 about his first DUI arrest in 2004. Now, a short two years later, he has a second DUI. To his credit, Phelps voluntarily entered a six-week in-patient treatment program. Is it doable?

Any in-patient treatment program has more to it than just "entering voluntarily." It has to do with a change in lifestyle, and, more often than not, a change in associates (called "friends"). However, if Phelps is serious, and he has good reason to be, he can make it "doable." He can again be a world-class swimmer as well as a world-class citizen. But he needs support! His swim coach and his discipline of early morning workouts with countless hours of pool time made him a champion. Let's hope his upcoming challenge involves a coach and self-discipline!

Will you maintain a discipline that leads you to be a citizen of good-standing?

February 23, 2015

After further review …

Trust figures prominently in any examination of our society's ethics in recent times. Parents, for example, trust teachers to help their children learn, and educators assume the principle of "in loco parentis," providing guidance in the absence of the legal guardians. So much of what happens in sports hinges on making the right choice, doing the right thing. Where our children are concerned we trust coaches and trainers as well.

Cut to Chicago, which had one of the most bitterly cold and snowbound winters in history. Yet the devastation of this brutal winter pales next to this humiliation: stripping the Jackie Robinson West team of its 2014 Little League U.S. Championship. JRW, the pride of Chicago's South Side, which lost the World Championship to South Korea in the Little League World Series at Williamsport, Pennsylvania, had won its playoff games up till then.

The cause of this removal was the fact that JRW team officials "knowingly fielded players who lived outside their team's established boundaries." Then those same adults tried to cover up their deception. A couple of neighboring districts weren't fielding a team, so the JRW manager, Darold Butler (the Butler did it?) recruited players he knew did not live in his district. Butler has been suspended and the District 4 supervisor, Michael Kelley, was also removed from his position. (By the way, officials from those neighboring districts were aware of the falsifications, but didn't speak up.)

And what about those 13 players, 11- and-12-year-olds who, according to one mother, "played their hearts out?" Of course it's not fair to them. But the comment of another parent—"Little League says they teach character and courage and this isn't an act of either"—misses the mark. Sorry, but responsibility for one's action (i.e., character) is exactly what is being taught and hopefully learned. While these 13 kids are blameless, they are subject to the consequences of choices made on their behalf. These lessons can serve them well in their personal and professional lives.

Are rules made simply to be broken or artfully bent? Haven't we seen enough of that, in sports and business? Yes, I'm sorry for these JRW kids, but they'll be OK. Resilience is the mantra of youth.

 Will you use "just do the right thing" as your mantra?

After further review …

As we tighten the lid on the year 2014 we highlight a theme that has dominated the sports world: "No more!" What drew the emphasis to this campaign was the rapt attention to the increased coverage of domestic violence and sexual assaults. I fail to understand such behavior since fortune dictated I would grow up in a family where these failures of self-control were unknown.

"No more!" domestic violence. There may always be disagreement among family members about how to raise their children. Psychologists assure us that chief among family issues will be money, sex and religion. But what about the method of disagreeing without being disagreeable? Does one have to be right or have his or her own way in a disagreement? Are compromise and an effort to get along passé? Can we learn to understand another's point of view without verbal or physical abuse? Sure we can.

"No more!" sexual assaults. Psychologists tell us sexual assaults are more about asserting power over another than achieving sexual satisfaction. The driving theme can simply be expressed, "It's all about me." The belief here is: that our existence on this planet should be governed by the question of what we can do for someone else. When one takes that approach, violence and assaults may disappear.

"No more!" trash-talking among players—both on and off the field. Trash-talking is just that: trash. None of us want to live or act like people with no value or goodness. It belittles any of us when we choose that behavior. It's a false sense of power. While that kind of talk has become ordinary today, it can be curtailed. It becomes the responsibility of every parent and every teacher to demand civilized and respectful language. There are over 1 million words in the English language; using the belittling minority of those occurs all too often.

We endeavor to teach athletes that their sport is one of respect. To attempt to defeat an opponent with the use of derogatory terms is the antithesis of the game itself. When trash-talking is directed at you, one of the healthiest responses is to simply walk away, denying the offender the sense of power they seek. Remember, "Whatsoever you do to the least of my brothers…"

Will you resolve to practice the "no more" approach in all you do in this coming year?

May 10, 2015

After further review …

With the "wrap" of the 2015 National Football League college draft, the final tally was 256 players selected. It is interesting to speculate how many will remain in the NFL for the projected average career of 3 1/2 years.

No one invites the question more bluntly than "Mr. Irrelevant," Gerald Christian, the Louisville Cardinal tight end taken dead last by the Arizona Cardinals. How long will his feathers stay red? Stay tuned!

In presentations to thousands of corporate audiences I often use the team-building theme: Don't give up on people too soon! As an example, I point out that Joe Montana was a third-round choice (No. 82 overall) of the San Francisco 49ers when he graduated from Notre Dame. But 49ers head coach Bill Walsh saw something in Montana, and he became a four-time Super Bowl winner and three-time MVP. Or how about New England Patriots quarterback Tom Brady, who was the 199th pick in the 2000 NFL draft? One-hundred ninety-eight players were chosen before Brady, whose still-active career with his original team has equaled Montana's Super Bowl achievements.

Sarah Thomas is the first female selected by the NFL to be an on-field official. She will serve as a line judge in the upcoming 2015 season. Thomas began football officiating in 1996, and worked her first varsity high school game in 1999. She was hired by Conference USA in 2000 and officiated her first major college game in 2007. By 2009 she was working a full college schedule of 11 games, and was selected for a postseason assignment.

Thomas officiated in the United Football League in 2010, and worked in the 2014 NFL preseason. Her "rookie" NFL regular season follows 19 years of experience on the field. Don't give up on people too soon!

My friend and colleague Johnny Grier has retired! His uniform number was 23— same as the years of his on-field NFL tenure. I was fortunate to have Grier assigned to our crew when he began in 1981. As crew chief, I asked him to be our "downfield referee" since, as a field judge, he was stationed some 25 yards from the line of scrimmage. His skill at that location was recognized by the NFL when he was selected to officiate Super Bowl XXII in 1988. He was assigned to the referee position the following season to become the first African-American to earn the title. His officiating career spanned half a century. The NFL and I will miss his wisdom and integrity.

 Will you help others progress by not giving up on them too soon?

3 COMPETENCE

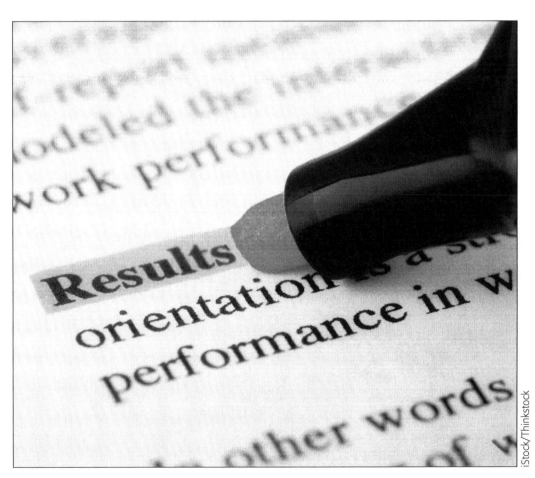

After further review …

Many sportswriters are calling it a plethora! The Kentucky Wildcats basketball team went 38-1 in 2014-15. While their goal was to be the first team in NCAA history to go 40-0, they lost in the NCAA semifinals to the Wisconsin Badgers.

"Well," say Kentucky fans, "wait till next year!" March Madness? Stay tuned.

The Wildcats had three freshmen (6-foot-6 Devin Booker, 6-10 Trey Lyles and 6-11 Karl-Anthony Towns), three sophomores (7-0 Dakari Johnson, and 6-6 twins Andrew and Aaron Harrison), and one junior (7-0 Willie Cauley-Stein). Sounds like a strong returning squad, doesn't it? Cauley-Stein is considered likely to be a "three and see ya" by forgoing his senior year.

But—and here's where the word "plethora" enters the picture—all seven of the above are skipping the remainder of their college educations to turn pro now! Towns, the 7-0 freshman, is projected to be the No. 1 draft selection. But two didn't even make their college starting lineup, yet believe they can qualify for a pro squad. Hmmm …

It is not unusual in this crazy NCAA/NBA system for those who spend only one year in college to go professional. In fact, Duke, which has been quite adamant against the "one-and-done" system, has three freshman players on this year's team opting to go pro. The practice today has been described by a veteran college coach as an effort to recruit the best player available even if he only intends to play for one year!

Is the term "student-athlete" passé? The NCAA staunchly defends its position that the "student" is first and the "athlete" second. Its maxim is that all athletes—superstar or otherwise—enter college to get an education qualifying them for future endeavors. Statistics show that only a small percentage of college athletes are successful at the professional level, so this presumed education is of major importance. Yet the demands on a Division I college athlete's time on the field or court are nearly double the time allotted for class attendance and study.

An NCAA spokesperson recently commented that the organization is not responsible for an athlete's academic progress at the Division I level, even though a GPA of 2.0 is required in determining an athlete's eligibility. Confused? Climb on board.

 Will you log in whether it should be student-athlete or athlete-student?

After further review …

A recent altercation between two very well-known college teams caught my attention. The ritual prior to every football game is preceded by a sportsmanlike handshake and a friendly greeting; except that didn't happen in this college game. A skirmish (kind word for "fighting/trash talking") broke out prior to a game between two college teams in the same conference. The meeting of the captains followed with one team's captains extending their hands only to be rebuffed by the other team's captains, who kept their hands at their side. Where was the coach?

Seems the coach was right there on the field, but failed to recognize this or take control of his team. The coach and his school were fined a five-figure dollar amount. The captain of the offending team was suspended for one game. The school and the coach have issued apologies saying we "did not live up to the standards that we set for ourselves." The player said he takes "full responsibility for my actions by letting my emotions get the best of me." The question of "scholar-athlete" becomes important. Many are suggesting that colleges allow players to play for their school without the "inconvenience" of pursuing an education. Not so from this view point.

Attending college and playing on sports teams, or representing the school in any form, is a privilege—not a right! Scholar-athletes are required to maintain an established grade-point average in order to compete. For this involvement they receive tuition, room and board, and a monetary stipend, not every athlete, but those who meet the qualifications of "superior talent." If there were no class attendance and its incumbent grade-point average required, what control would a college have to ensure the athlete meets its citizenship and sportsmanship standards?

Even today with these regulations in place, there is a major concern about some athletes who commit acts of misbehavior, e.g., sexual assaults, thievery, DUIs, etc. To this writer the use of the word athlete is misplaced. The only way an individual should be able to use the title athlete is if he or she lives up to the highest levels of citizenship, scholarship and sportsmanship. The singular fact of being a talented player should not carry the title of athlete for one who breaches those values.

Will you agree: schools need to continue requiring standards of good citizenship and sportsmanship and class attendance from every athlete in their programs?

After further review …

It has always been this writer's belief that pride counts for something.

The old saw states "If you don't stand for something, you'll fall for anything." Being proud of your effort is what life is all about. Enron, WorldCom, Adelphia, Bernie Madoff and the like are examples of greed overtaking self-pride. As someone said, "Decent people don't do things like that."

In the sports world we see the lack of pride take its toll. As this football season comes to a close, some teams are playing out their schedule without a bowl or playoff opportunity. For players on those teams, their effort to perform at their best is a matter of pride. A mnemonic dissection of the word P-R-I-D-E might employ these words: P=Power; R=Responsibility; I=Integrity; D=Determination; E=Excellence. We'll save a more complete explanation for another time.

What prompted this column/blog was a recent report indicating that U.S. teens lag in international tests. This was followed by the news that Asian students outperform their global peers—and scored well above Americans—in tests of reading, math and science proficiency. We (the good old USA) have always proclaimed ourselves the greatest nation on the planet. Not so, when U.S. teenagers rank 26th in math, 17th in reading, and 21st is science—among 15-year-olds in 34 countries. As one comedian said, "Maybe we fall behind in the Three Rs, since only one of them actually begins with an R."

The PISA (Program for International Student Assessment) is "aimed at what students really know and how they can apply their knowledge to the real world."

This is not an effort to belittle anyone responsible for the education of our youth, but simply a wake-up call. How do we place a greater emphasis on our youth taking pride in everything they do? To develop pride in one's effort may be the answer to improving those scores. Obviously, no one person or treatise would be able to solve this problem. But let's try this idea: "You play to win the game," said former NFL head coach Herm Edwards. By that he meant you give your best effort every time.

Or as the legendary Grantland Rice once wrote: "It's not whether you win or lose, but how you play the game." The emphasis is on giving one's best performance with the idea that if one does so—every time—the odds are success will happen. The effort to succeed will serve you well in all that you do. As parents, teachers and coaches we need to inspire the value of performance. Take pride in your performance and the results are inevitable.

 Will you reward effort as long as it is the best effort from that person?

December 23, 2013

After further review …

As we near the end of 2013, celebrating Christmas and the holiday season, there is no doubt that scores of sports-themed stories are swirling in the winter air waiting to be told. The TUNNEYSIDE of Sports is always on the lookout for the transformative and thought-provoking tale that helps us add character and purpose to everyday living. But in the genuine spirit of the season, allow me the privilege to simply stand back with all of you and appreciate that gift that unites us. Nowhere is it better expressed than in the lyrics to Barbra Streisand's "Here's to Life," written by Phyllis Molinary and Artie Butler. Please take a moment to absorb them and reflect on the deep value of that gift, life itself. "L'Chaim."

> *No complaints and no regrets*
> *I still believe in chasing dreams and placing bets*
> *And I have learned that all you give is all you get*
> *So give it all you got.*
>
> *I had my share, I drank my fill*
> *And even though I'm satisfied, I'm hungry still*
> *To see what's down another road, beyond a hill*
> *And do it all again.*
>
> *So here's to life*
> *And every joy it brings*
> *Here's to life*
> *To dreamers and their dreams.*
>
> *Funny how the time just flies*
> *How love can go from hellos to sad goodbyes*
> *And leave you with the memories you've memorized*
> *To keep your winters warm.*
>
> *But there's no yes in yesterday*
> *And who knows what tomorrow brings, or takes away*
> *As long as I'm still in the game, I want to play*
> *For laughs, for life, for love.*

So here's to life, and every joy it brings—Here's to life!

 Will you give it all you got no matter what the end result may be?

After further review …

Is cheerleading a sport?

That energetic art has been around almost as long as sport itself. In the beginning, before the choreographed squads wearing varsity-letter sweaters appeared, there were guys and gals basically jumping up and down and hollering for their team. But oh my, how that instinct has developed.

Pretty girls with shapely legs and exuberant boys with megaphones (remember those?) have evolved into tight-knit teams, performing athletic maneuvers that require serious training and conditioning, exposing them to risks never dreamed of by the raccoon-cap-and-saddle-shoes crowd. Many believe today's cheerleaders are not getting the respect they deserve.

"I think it should be considered a sport," said Kristine Durfee, the cheer coach at Red Bluff High School. "They take tumbling classes and gymnastics. They are athletes and are required to perform like athletes."

Desiree Turner, cheer coach at Oakland High School, agrees. "They practice year-round and put in as much work as a football or basketball player," she said. "They do stunts. I require them to go to cheerleading camp so they can learn how to do it safely. We do lots of fundraising so they can go to camp."

Well, the "sport" has certainly changed from a few girls who dance in short skirts with pom-poms, with or without music, to today's gymnastic drill teams inciting the crowd to yell and scream for their players on the field or court. (By the way, how come we don't see cheerleaders at baseball games, tennis matches or swim meets?)

Now steps up the American Association of Cheerleading Coaches and Administrators to declare its parameters by stating: "Cheerleading does not meet the requirements of being a sport because the primary purpose is not competition; it's raising school unity at athletic functions." Most state interscholastic federations do not sanction cheerleading.

In the meantime the TUNNEYSIDE admires the school spirit generated by young men and women who make the effort to provide positive school climates. That enthusiasm is contagious and can affect the entire student body. My experience has shown me that these activities give every student a sense of pride in their school. Further, the value of any group working together can serve each participant in life's future endeavors.

 Will you chime-in on whether cheerleading is a sport?

August 10, 2014

After further review …

Much of my adult working life has placed me in the position of making decisions about others. Of course, I had decisions to make during childhood—mostly personal, type of clothing to wear or buy, kind of ice cream cone preferred, etc.—mundane choices for what I wanted or needed. This column/blog is focused more on decisions we make involving others. Although research tells us that two of the most difficult decisions an adult must make are choosing a mate and buying a home, this topic is about how to consider what process to use when making decisions about others.

As a teacher, coach and school administrator I was faced, daily, with decisions that could shape the lives of others. Many of these decisions were of a disciplinary nature, which was the result of a student's wrong action. Some were minor and seemingly easily corrected. Others were more serious to the point of suspension or expulsion. In every case an examination of the issue had to be carefully considered. A decision formed hastily and without a thorough thought process could have an adverse effect.

My father, a former teacher and school administrator, taught me three principles of decision making. First, consider what is best for that person. In other words, as a decision maker one needs to know how the affected person will respond. The goal is helping that person learn and respond successfully. It is often said: Forget what hurt you, but never forget what it taught you. The true definition of discipline is learning, not punishment.

Second, how will your decision affect the group? People can learn from another's mistake so your decision is important for those surrounded by the accused. Further, the strength of your decision can affect other's thought processes. Their reaction(s) may be positive or negative based on your decision.

Thirdly, what would your decision be, if this person were your son or daughter? We certainly want the best for our own and not let our decision destroy one's self-esteem or self-confidence. Yet, a wrongful deed needs to be corrected.

This topic will be followed in the future with decision making in the business world.

 Will you give thoughtful consideration to the process you follow in making decisions?

After further review …

In part one of the TUNNEYSIDE approach to making decisions, a prescription was offered for creating a positive effect on disciplinary actions affecting others. Taught to me by my father, it had a 3-tenet doctrine asking the questions:

- What is best for the individual?
- What is best for the group/community?
- What decision would you make if this were your child?

In sports officiating, other approaches may be necessary. Sport officials are required to call the game/match according to established rules and procedures. In a perfect world could sports events be conducted by allowing the participants to call their own infractions? We did that, of course, when we were kids playing on the playground or in the street. Both sides used their own sense of fair play. Hmmm, how did that all change when we grew up?

Dr. David Redish, a professor in the department of neuroscience at the University of Minnesota, authored the book, "The Mind within the Brain" where he describes his decision-making systems. One part he calls "deliberate," i.e., after careful thought, involves the process that correct and meaningful decisions are made through deliberation. However, sports officials, more often than not, need to make game-type decisions on the spot. Redish calls these types "procedural." Perhaps another term might be "reflexive," meaning the making of a decision in a procedural way through reflexes.

To make decisions based on reflexes, every sports official must have a thorough knowledge of the rules. This means not only committing the written word in the rule book to memory, i.e., rote; but also knowing the spirit of the rule. Add to that an understanding of why the rule is there and the purpose it serves. "Knowing the game" will also serve every official well. Does the official understand the manner in which the game is played, i.e., formations, styles of play, etc.? Styles and formations are dynamic and often change. Officials must do that as well.

The purpose of officiating is not just to ensure the players play within the established rules, but also to keep the game moving with celerity, thereby making it interesting for fans. Further, officials must conduct themselves in a professional manner to uphold the integrity of the game. Stay tuned for part three coming next week.

 Will you thoroughly prepare in order to make informed decisions accurate

4 COURAGE

iStock/Thinkstock

After further review …

With the completion of the 79th Masters golf tournament on Sunday, the age-old question is asked once more: How does one qualify to receive such a prestigious invitation? The truth is that 99-plus percent of those playing golf today will never be invited to participate.

But ask any of those legions of golfers, and they will tell you that simply to play Augusta National would be a dream come true, never mind the green jacket. There are 19 routes to that coveted invitation. So, how did a professional golfer ranked 117th by Official World Golf get one, and who is he?

His name is Erik Compton, 35, born and raised in Miami, and he has played golf since he was 12. At age 18, he was the top-ranked junior golfer in the United States, and later became a two-time All-American at the University of Georgia coached by Chuck Haack—or "Hacker," as he is known by the six—yes, six—professional protégés who played in this year's Masters. But Haack's tutelage alone did not qualify Compton for an invitation to play in the event he had dreamed of all his life. Stay tuned.

Compton's second-place tie in the 2014 U.S. Open at Pinehurst No. 2 did! And for that he earned $789,330, his biggest win ever. With that tidy sum, you'd think Compton might have celebrated by taking a cruise or a vacation. Nope—Erik played in the Travelers Championship in Crowell, Connecticut, the very next week, which gave him the chance to show up at Hartford Hospital and visit heart transplant patients.

You see, Compton, who walked the Augusta National terrain last week, has had two heart transplants. His first was in 1992 at age 12 due to cardiomyopathy. The second was in 2008, at age 29. If you're keeping score at home, Compton played this year's Masters with his third heart.

His appearance at the Hartford hospital was no surprise. Photographers had followed Compton there, but he avoided them, saying he preferred private time with patients. One of them, Shawn Fullard, was preparing to undergo her second and had lost considerable weight. Compton told her his weight dropped to 129 pounds following his second procedure, and assured her the weight will come back. He encouraged her to "stay strong;" then, he autographed a golf glove for her.

 Will you have the heart to follow your dreams even under trying circumstances?

After further review …

During a recent high school girls' basketball game, both coaches told their players to "play to lose"! C'mon, man! The players were ordered to lose in order not to face a stronger opponent in the upcoming playoffs. The names of these two coaches and their schools are not mentioned here as their identities are not the point.

Who's to blame for this ethical failure? The two coaches, for starters. But where were the school administrators? Should players be accountable? Probably not—their first duty is to obey their coach. Credit the game officials, who witnessed this flagrant disregard for the integrity of the game and tried to intervene. They then followed up with a game report to the proper authorities.

Several egregious methods were used to "throw" the game: free throws intentionally missed, players intentionally failing to get the ball into their front court within 10 seconds (the resulting violation causing a turnover), one player attempting to shoot at the opponent's basket and various other intentional turnovers.

Both coaches have been suspended and will not be permitted to coach during the 2015-16 school year. Both teams have been banned for the remainder of the season and disqualified for possible postseason games. Both schools were fined.

"You play to win the game! Hello! You play to win the game," said the always passionate former New York Jets head coach Herm Edwards midway through the 2002 NFL season, when the Jets were losing. A reporter had mused that the season "may be a lost cause," Herm continued, "That's the great thing about sports. You don't play just to play it! I don't care if you don't have any wins; you play to win." In that 2002 season the Jets finished 9-7 and made the playoffs.

Coaches are there to encourage players to always give their best effort. The main ingredient in the word encourage is "courage." What better place than sports can help a young person muster the strength to "keep on keepin' on?"

 Will you help others who may be facing a difficult situation to find the courage within?

After further review …

The 2015 Special Olympics World Games recently concluded, after gathering 6,500 athletes, 2,000 coaches and 3,000 volunteers from 165 countries in Los Angeles. For nine days 500,000 spectators were treated to the efforts and achievements of these special athletes.

You missed it? Unfortunately, so did I. But, even from a distance I could feel the uplifting spirit of Special Olympics, which began for me in the early 1970s and continued through the '80s in California. It has left me with an undying appreciation for these athletes.

It was a kind, but curious, invitation sent to me in 1972 to be a "celebrity" participant in the state games held at UCLA. I had seen wonderful athletes, up close and personal, since I was about 5. But what I was seeing in these special athletes, young and old, competing in a variety of sports contests, was a new definition of the word "competition." I remember in particular an adult male of 26, with no use of either hand or one leg, pushing his wheelchair backward 25 yards, finishing third with a smile on his face as if he had just won the Indy 500. BTW, it took him eight minutes to travel those 25 yards!

In my book, "It's the Will, Not the Skill," which extols the trials and efforts of former NFL player and head coach Herm Edwards, I found inspiration in the example of special athletes everywhere. Indeed, it is expressed in the title; while dissimilar in many aspects to those with developmental challenges, Edwards' path to NFL success emphasized the will to attempt it. That very same will employed by my "wheelchair Al Unser" those many years ago.

From the sidelines at a number of these special games, I have admired not only the competitive spirit of special athletes, but the sportsmanlike attitude of each. At one high jump event, competitors who were waiting their turn vigorously clapped and cheered for another competitor who cleared the bar, and consoled another whose attempt fell short. I would have liked to have seen that same sportsmanlike spirit recently from a MLB player, whose towering fly ball was turned from a home run into an out by his competing outfielder's spectacular catch atop the wall. Just a tip-o'-the-cap would do.

 Will you follow the Special Olympics motto, "Let me win; but if I cannot win, let me be brave in the attempt!"

After further review …

The first half of February highlighted an interesting parallel. It began with the announcement by the University of Missouri's star defensive end, Michael A. Sam Jr., that he was "coming out."

That's a term in common use this time of year when college undergrads leave behind their senior year to enter the NFL draft. This was not the case with Sam; he was telling the world that he is gay.

Some in the athletic world accepted it. Some denounced it. And others proclaimed that in the NFL it would be too much of a distraction. The opinion here is that it would only be a distraction if some want to make it so. Sam was co-player of the year in the Southeastern Conference in 2013.

His announcement was a bold move, indeed, coming just prior to the 2014 NFL combine, when all players interested in playing pro ball arrive in Indianapolis to be timed, tested, examined, and interviewed. Will Sam be judged by his sexual identity, or on his ability as a player?

We move from that question to the ESPN documentary film "51 Dons," which aired on that network the second week of the month. The University of San Francisco Dons went undefeated with a record of 9-0 in 1951, but didn't make it to a bowl game. Miami's Orange Bowl invited them, but with the stipulation that the Dons leave behind their two African American players, Ollie Matson and Burl Toler.

The '51 Dons stood strong as a band of brothers and refused to allow racism do what no opponent had done. They turned down that bowl bid, a bold move indeed. But would those Dons be judged by their willingness to play along, or by their human decency?

Matson became a Hall-of-Fame player who in 1959 was traded to the Los Angeles Rams for nine players. Toler became the NFL's first black official, and handled the inevitable slurs and racial epithets with dignity. I know firsthand since he and I worked on the NFL field together.

The USA is still the land of the free and the home of the brave. It is hoped that Sam's bravery will meet, as time goes by, a response that honors those very words we use to describe ourselves.

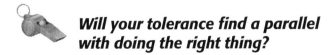

Will your tolerance find a parallel with doing the right thing?

After further review …

During the XXII Winter Olympics in Sochi, Russia, we heard one of the many NBC announcers invoke the term "clutch performances," while at the same time chiding some of the Olympic athletes for failure to deliver on their high expectations.

It begs the question of anyone in competition: Are you a clutch performer? Can you depend on your skills to be successful, when it comes to what is called a defining moment? Can others rely on you to come through in the clutch?

Having been on the NFL field with "clutch" quarterbacks (Bart Starr, Johnny Unitas, Joe Namath, Joe Montana, Steve Young, Roger Staubach, John Elway, Terry Bradshaw, Jim Kelly, and Dan Marino being the cream of that crop), I saw them consistently come through to win games. Time after time in critical final drives I'd see these exceptional players call the play in the huddle, inspiring the T*E*A*M around them to grab victory on the next snap of the ball.

So what does it take to come through in the clutch? Here is the TUNNEYSIDE take on that question: First, it takes your will. Simply and briefly, it's the desire, the passion and the never-quit belief that you will rise to the challenge! Second, prepare thoroughly! There is no substitute! As legendary Los Angeles Rams Hall of Famer Merlin Olsen said, "The will to prepare is more important than the will to win!"

Third, you need focus. One must concentrate on the task ahead and block out all distractions. Many call that being "in the zone." When you are in the zone, everything seems to happen in slow motion. Fourth, courage is called for. You must be willing to take a chance and risk failure. It takes courage to enjoy being competitive. Your courage will often bring out the best in you.

Talent may make an appearance in a clutch scenario. Clutch performers will often have no idea where they learned the execution for the game-winning move. Instead, it's the elements of will, preparation, focus and courage that puts one in the class of clutch players.

 Will you develop the will to be a clutch performer?

After further review …

With the NBA and NHL playoffs going full blast, let us consider the relationship between the word "blast" and the term "mind games." Players try to get into their opponents' heads with verbal taunts. Or blasts, if you will. This is not something new. Talking to your opponent during the heat of battle has been a practice since the very first kickoff, opening pitch, or dropped puck. And mind games start even before the game begins.

Did I see it during my tenure in the NFL? Sure did. Some years back the verbal taunting was also racially demeaning, as minorities began to participate at the highest levels of professional sports. Tolerance for racial taunting has diminished, thankfully. The predominance of microphones and cameras has something to do with that. So does the attitude of the NFL, when it establishes a rule that would penalize a player 15 yards for the use of the "N-word." Good riddance to racism on the playing fields.

Mind games exist is most relationships. Can they be positive in any way? Sure they can. Motivational tools often rely on some form of psychological manipulation. But a mind game that is used to distract one from his or her intended purpose can't be described as positive motivation. Imagine a catcher slyly telling a batter, "Sometimes our pitcher's curve ball doesn't break, so watch out." I remember hitting a rare single as a high school player and then taking my lead off first base. So happy to be there, I got chatty with the first baseman and lost my concentration. Next thing I knew I was picked off. I'd forgotten my dad's advice, "Be friendly to an opponent, but don't talk or listen to him."

Trash-talking by today's professional players has not only escalated, but has filtered down to the college, high school and Little League levels. Derogatory comments are intended to incite an opponent into a hostile response. That response is where the damage gets done; focus and purpose can be lost. Boxing trainers remind their fighters to battle with purpose, not anger. Losing one's temper is the fastest way to make the goal disappear. Renowned martial arts artist and actor Chuck Norris said, "People are like steel. When they lose their temper, they lose their worth."

 Will you maintain your personal worth when being attacked with mind games?

5 FAMILY

After further review …

With football season now underway, the TUNNEYSIDE thought you might like this story about junior league football from Steve Young, the Hall of Fame former quarterback of the San Francisco 49ers, who tells this story about his early days as a football player:

"I have often been told that I am a quarterback with the mindset of a running back. People always commented on my ability to scramble, yet that wasn't always my style. All professional athletes retain vivid memories of events that helped mold them into the players they are today. The following story marks the beginning of my scrambling techniques.

"I was nine years old and playing in a competitive game of Pop Warner football. I played running back for the North Mianus Indians (Riverside, Connecticut). We were playing against the Belle Haven Buzzards and our quarterback tossed me the ball. I took a few tentative steps and while I was trying to figure out where I should run, I was tackled. It was an illegal neck tackle that threw me on my back and knocked the wind out of me.

"As I tried to catch my breath, I saw my parents run onto the field towards me. I thought, 'Oh, gosh, please Mom, go back to the sideline.' See, it was okay to have my dad run onto the field, but it was certainly not cool to have my mother come charging over with him. When they finally reached me, and much to my surprise, as my father bent down to see how I was doing, my mother leapt over me, ran several more yards and grabbed the kid who had tackled me. She picked him up off the ground by his jersey, she shook him and shouted: 'Don't you ever neck-tackle!'

"Needless to say, I was fine, but I'm not sure that kid ever recovered from the shock. From that moment forth, I learned to scramble, and quickly. I lived in fear of being tackled and had visions of my mother storming onto the field to reprimand the tackler. So, through a little motivation from Mom, I learned that there are tremendous advantages to scrambling and avoiding tacklers."

Will you learn proper techniques in playing any game?

After further review …

As the youth foundation that bears my name begins its 23rd year (founded June, 1993), we are grateful to its board of directors. We appreciate equally all those in our community who continue to support the Jim Tunney Youth Foundation's mission to serve the youth of the Monterey Peninsula. In that time, the JTYF, a 501c3 non-profit, has made grants to youth organizations in excess of a quarter-million dollars.

Our primary funding has been generated by our Sportsnights, an evening dedicated to the interaction between celebrity sports stars and local kids, along with their coaches, teachers and other significant adults. Such celebrated figures as Joe Montana, Herm Edwards, Ronnie Lott, Steve Young, Don Shula and Johnny Miller, among others, have each donated an evening of their time, at no cost to the foundation, to speak to the 400-plus audience, each providing a unique example of personal growth through dedication to their dreams and goals. These messages are uniformly positive and supportive.

The 2014 sports star was Andrew Luck, currently the starting quarterback for the Indianapolis Colts. His message was: "If any of you have aspirations of playing in the NFL, let me remind you that the average length of a player's career is three and a half years. So, should that be your length of time on the field, you need to have a plan to support yourself for the 60-plus years of your life. For that reason, I return to school (Stanford University) every off-season to learn all that I can about my field of study (architectural design)."

Wardell Stephen "Steph" Curry impresses the TUNNEYSIDE with a similar attitude and demeanor. Curry, the point guard for the Golden State Warriors and the NBA's 2015 MVP, is a graduate of Davidson College, a small (1700) liberal arts college located in North Carolina. Curry is grounded by his faith and family—led by his dad, Deli, a former NBA player, and his mom, Sonya, who helped Steph understand that hiding behind sunglasses (indoors) and headphones would diminish him as an individual. Steph remains vibrant on and off the court following that advice.

In a recent newspaper article, the writer said Curry would not be welcomed at the school in which he teaches because most kids who dream of playing in the NBA don't have the nurturing background of an NBA father. The TUNNEYSIDE respectfully disagrees. Curry, who once was 5' 6" and "slow afoot" (according to his mother), has a work ethic second-to-none. How many players practice bouncing two basketballs simultaneously before every game and shoot 10 shots from 10 different spots outside the 3-point arc every day? If you're keeping score, that's 100 shots every day. Yes, the JTYF would welcome #30 Steph Curry to join its sportsnight alumni.

 Will you admire Curry's work ethic and devotion to faith and family?

After further review …

It's a rhetorical question you should be familiar with if you have youngsters, "Can't we just let 'em play?"

But for many parents who subject their children to the frantic world of media attention, ignoring it has reached a crisis point. There are too many examples today of parents "pushing" kids to extremes in search of financial rewards in the sports world. A father creates a website, stuffed with photos, videos and stats of his son; it's as if he were a college and pro recruit. The lad's in the sixth grade. Just let him play!

"It's ridiculous" said one sports psychologist. He's right, but his assessment doesn't go far enough. It's obscene! Overzealous parents have been exploiting their kids in many venues for years. Hollywood, California and Nashville, Tennessee are inundated with young people wanting to be in movies and the music industries. Burlesque queen Gypsy Rose Lee was a famous example of a daughter who never achieved the level of fame that her relentlessly manipulative mother Rose dreamed of for young "Louise Havick."

In the sports world, parents have been just as selfishly driven, and we may now be observing a breaking point. The sixth-grade boy mentioned above is being groomed, it would appear, as the next Peyton Manning. His parents have hired a quarterback coach and are sending him to QB school to get him noticed—at age 11! Certainly, as parents, we love to see our sons and daughters perform well on the sports field. Further, we want to support and encourage their athletic dreams. But we have to recognize the difference between a parental fantasy and a kid's natural progression through the games he or she loves to play.

Youth sports are a great way to teach youngsters the value of hard work, overcoming adversity, and working together with others. These values are available to any kid who participates at any level, starting in backyards and sandlots. So let them go play, with no coaches or referees. Let them make up their own games with their own rules and just have fun!

 Will you allow your youngster to grow and become the person he/she wants to be?

After further review …

An ad that the NFL is currently running on national network and cable television proclaims "Football is family!" Its purpose, of course, is to encourage the whole family to watch the games.

The game of football has been a big part of my life as well as that of my family's. I have no exact fix on when it started, but I can't remember when it wasn't part of our family's fabric. My father, Jim Sr., was an outstanding high school and college player, and then a high school football coach at Lincoln (L.A.), where he coached Kenny Washington, the first African-American player for the Los Angeles Rams.

My dad's footprint as a football official left a large one for me to fill. But I took my first step at the age of 5 or 6, when I accompanied him to high school and college games he officiated. My officiating history, therefore, is now in its eighth decade as I continue working for the NFL as an observer/mentor to today's NFL officials. Football is family!

As today's game has become more physical than ever before with the size, strength and speed of its athletes, today's officials must, and do, maintain a physical, mental and emotional strength to keep pace. There is no denying the physicality of the game, with the credo that "Ya gotta knock somebody down," and the injuries that occur. But everyone involved recognizes the need to minimize injuries of every description. Every team considers its players a family, with their welfare of paramount importance.

Fans rarely pay much attention to the officials on the field—until controversy is introduced. But here's something to note: During October, all NFL on-field officials use pink whistles and wear pink armbands in support of Breast Cancer Awareness month. This has been an annual occurrence for several years. Further, officials work in their communities to help raise funds for charitable causes. Why do game officials do this? Is this a part of their job?

While certainly not required, it's the type of ancillary characteristic the NFL looks for in its officiating candidates—those who are best able to represent the league. The morning of every NFL game, the crew of seven NFL officials gathers before breakfast in a special meeting called a "devotional." Anyone on the crew might lead a discussion that touches upon their gratitude for this officiating opportunity, striving for the best job that can be done, and prayerful consideration of their brethren and others who may be ill or suffering.

 Will you uphold your family with some of the same values found in a football family?

After further review …

After enduring a shaky relationship, Harry (Billy Crystal) and Sally (Meg Ryan) reconnected on New Year's Eve while the perennial question "Should auld acquaintance be forgot …" rang out. Harry interjects to Sally, "I never understood what that means. I mean, should we forget our old friends, or what?" Sally doesn't have a clue! Two of my auld acquaintances left us this year, but their memories will remain forever.

Hollywood Park Race Track closed on Dec. 22 after 75 years. My brother Peter was born the same year it opened, and started working at Hollywood Park as a parking lot attendant while in college.

After graduating he served as a steward and then assistant to the chairman of the board. Peter's successful career lengthened at Golden Gate Fields (Albany, CA), where he has been the general manager for more than 30 years. His success in racing, I'm sure he would agree, is only surpassed by our father, Jim Sr. Dad began his work in thoroughbred racing in the mid-'40s after a successful career as an educator and sports official.

Jim Sr. was a steward at Hollywood Park, Santa Anita, and Del Mar race tracks for 20 years. He had never ridden a thoroughbred horse, or any other horse for that matter, and yet earned the respect of real horsemen—owners, trainers, and jockeys alike—with his quick study, his warm personality and his good judgment. Dad died on July 5, 1965, on his way home from Hollywood Park after a full card of eight races that day. A fellow steward was driving him home when Dad had a massive heart attack in the car. Dad was 59!

The other significant closure for me happened, Dec. 23 when the San Francisco 49ers played their final regular season game at Candlestick Park.

I was honored to have been the referee in the first 'Niners game there on Aug. 8, 1971, against the Cleveland Browns. Officiating so many memorable games there, I had the privilege of sharing the turf with John Brodie, Joe Montana, and Steve Young as well as many other legendary players.

Of course, Jan. 10, 1982 stands out. I was the referee in the game that featured "The Catch," now part of the NFL's timeless lore, that allowed the 49ers to defeat the Dallas Cowboys and go on to their first Super Bowl.

Quarterback Montana still claims "Whadda mean 'The Catch?' It's called 'The Throw!' It was my throw that made that play work, not the catch!" Joe and Dwight Clark have a great laugh about that. Whatever it is called, the 49ers fans believe it stands out as the best game ever played at the 'Stick. But closure arrives for everything, and life moves on.

 Will you keep your memories sacred, but continue to move forward in life?

After further review …

"You play the hand you're dealt" means you don't complain about not having an optimal situation, but instead just deal with things as they are. While this old saw may make more sense if you are playing a game of cards, it certainly applies to life situations.

It can mean seeing the glass as half-full instead of half-empty. It reminds us of Johnny Mercer's famous lyrics "Ya gotta accentuate the positive and eliminate the negative." It recalls an ancient Japanese proverb's useful suggestion that "You fall seven times but stand up eight." It asks each of us to quit grousing about our life's circumstances.

A case in point might be supplied by the Denver Broncos after their sound defeat by the Seattle Seahawks in Super Bowl XLVIII. It also applies to all the other NFL teams that did not, for whatever reasons, finish as Lombardi Trophy winners. Collectively, they may now look forward with hope and promise toward the 2014 NFL season.

But that's not really the story here. The comments today concern Demaryius Thomas, No. 88, wide receiver for the Broncos, who shared the unexpected and deeply disappointing outcome of the game with his teammates. But then, ever since Thomas was born he has faced a lifetime of the unexpected. By various reports he was a shy, withdrawn child in a troubled situation.

Thomas was just 11 when his mother and grandmother were arrested and convicted of charges of "conspiracy to possess with intent to distribute crack cocaine." They are still serving 20-year sentences in a federal correctional institution and are not expected to be released until 2017. Into that parental vacuum stepped his Aunt Shirley and Uncle James Brown.

Aunt Shirley and Uncle James sent Thomas to church, enrolled him in sports, and cheered for him at West Laurens High School in Dexter, GA. where he excelled in athletics. His GPA, his character, and his citizenship were strong enough for him to be offered scholarships to Duke, Georgia, and Georgia Tech, which he chose to attend with a major in management. Drafted 22nd by the Broncos, he scored a 34 (the upper most echelon) on the NFL Combine's Wonderlic Cognitive Ability Test.

In the first quarter of the Super Bowl, Thomas separated his shoulder, yet went on to catch 14 passes to surpass Dan Ross, Jerry Rice, Deion Branch and Wes Welker's record of 11. He didn't let his fan club down in Tallahassee.

 How will you play the hand you are dealt?

After further review …

I am often asked why I write about sports. My answer is simple: the world of sports offers me an endless opportunity to transform ethical issues into positive messages for productive living. My background and training as a teacher prepared me well for this practice, and I've had the good fortune to be well acquainted with highly visible athletes whose personal triumphs and challenges resonate with a wide audience.

You may not know about your plumber's latest brush with the law, or the plumbing code, but everybody knows what's up with the players on their favorite team. Unfortunately, the good things that many do are often overshadowed by the not-so-good.

Recently I was in an audience where the speaker asked, "What is the hallmark of sports?" It was a rhetorical question aiming for a variety of answers. The predominant response: family and team. The terms are interchangeable in my mind, since I firmly believe a family is—or certainly should function as—a team. I define "team" as "Together Everyone Accomplishes More." In order for a family to do that, each member must do his or her part to live and work together.

Sports teams are a family. Band/orchestra members are a family. Cast members in a play are a family. Each is a diverse collection of individuals, but the inclusion of each member is vital to the success of that organization. Likewise, the personality and convictions of family members may be dissimilar, but each one must feel (and be made to feel) part of that group in order for that member, as well as the team, to be productive.

The speaker also mentioned another word attached to sports: courage. It does take courage—one might call it "bravery," "pluck," or "valor"—to step onto the court, field or stage. Each individual who does so will have a better chance, if they feel part of that organization. Courage is fed by inclusion, not by isolation from a common goal. Self-belief is aided immeasurably by a sense of team unity. Those who have it are able to deal with anger, discomfort and intimidation better. The fear of failing is diminished. Put into clearer perspective: it is one of the stepping stones to success. Or as Don Quixote proclaimed famously: "If you'll only be true to this glorious quest, your heart will lie peaceful and calm …"

 Will you search for that inner strength that unity can bring?

6 INTEGRITY

After further review …

The final episode of the TUNNEYSIDE triad on making decisions deals with professionalism and integrity. The first segment, you will recall, dealt with creating a positive effect in cases of disciplinary action. The second described decisions that were mainly deliberate versus reflexive—reflexive being the kind game officials would make. The difference between a decision that involves sitting around a table and debating the pros and cons of an issue is vastly different than those decisions made "while the engine is running."

In the heat of an athletic contest, there is neither time nor appropriateness for "discussion." Game officials want to be—and must be—accurate and precise in every decision. They are being judged and critiqued by fans, coaches and players on every action or inaction. Further, in most professional sports, there is a fail-safe system called replay. The value of replay notwithstanding, an action-type game is designed to operate by the decisions of players, coaches and officials; none of whom is in infallible. Mistakes will occur.

In football, for example, every play is designed to be a success. Coaches choose plays that will work and players practice those plays to ensure they will succeed. If each play worked as it were designed and coaches and players executed as intended, game officials would officiate "the perfect game." But, that ain't gonna happen! That's why it's called a game!

The professionalism of officials is vital to maintain a high level of enjoyment. The officials must be at their best at all times, even when the game is not. During a game, coaches and players, although professional in their approach, may lose their cool in the heat of the contest. But the officials must not.

Professionalism starts with the approach of officials preparing themselves mentally, physically, emotionally and spiritually. Yes, spiritually, but more in the metaphysical sense than religious. Officials must maintain an attitude of positivity with an enthusiastic state of mind at all times. If, or when, abuse arises from fans, coaches or players, officials must rise above it and never respond in kind. It is their task to keep the game under control no matter what the circumstance.

Moreover, it is the officials' job to possess a level of impartiality and honesty. The utmost in integrity is the guiding force in any game.

 Will you maintain a high level of professionalism and integrity in whatever you do?

November 30, 2014

After further review …

Several months after refereeing Super Bowl XI on Jan. 9, 1977, I happened to see John Madden, the former Oakland Raiders head coach. The Raiders had defeated the Minnesota Vikings 32-14. Coach Madden was wearing his imposing Super Bowl XI ring given to him along with the players and appropriate team personnel as a symbol of their victory.

I had known John both on and off the field for several years and felt comfortable kidding with him. So I said, "John, that's a magnificent ring, but I didn't get one. I mean, you and I were on that Rose Bowl field for the same three hours and 15 minutes, yet you received that beautiful ring, and the NFL gave me this Timex. Why the difference?"

Without hesitation Madden said, "'Cause you don't care who wins!" Wow! That was a bit startling, but very true. As an NFL official responsible for the precise operation of the game, which team won was never important to me; properly officiating the game was!

A newspaper article with the headline "NBA conspiracy theories: Long shot or layups" caught my attention. The tenor of the story (I've seen this before) was that the NBA covertly controls which teams will end up in the playoffs by influencing the officiating. Ridiculous! I know many current NBA officials and many others over the years. Bashing the integrity of officiating is uncalled for.

Having officiated both football and basketball for over 40 years, it is apparent that officiating the game of professional basketball in today's style of play is incredibly difficult. With 7-foot, 250-pound guys charging, blocking, dunking and rebounding, it is often a contest more suited to the NFL field. To suggest that the NBA attempts to subvert rule enforcement so that certain teams progress through to the finals carries the word "theory" all the way to surrealism.

The days of "Donaghygate," circa 2007, are over. Tim Donaghy was a 13-year NBA official who was convicted and served a jail sentence following his conviction on federal gambling and conspiracy charges. Today's NBA officials have only one interest in mind: to officiate the game impartially. To suggest otherwise is farcical.

 Will you make your decisions based on your honest appraisal of the situation?

November 1, 2015

After further review …

The fall season is the time for cross country running. Overshadowed by more crowd-pleasing sports at all levels of play from high school through the pro ranks, cross country is often considered a "minor" sport! There's no question it lacks spectator appeal. Courses range in length from 2½ miles and beyond (depending on the age and sex of competitors), and fans tend to cluster at the start and finish lines. In between are long stretches of inhospitable trail without aid stations or camera crews, and runners tick those miles off in huffing, puffing solitude. It may not have the "sizzle" of football or soccer, but you might check out Kevin Costner's latest film "McFarland" to get an idea of what that sport can do for youngsters.

In a recent cross country state championship meet, "Zeke" we'll call him (to protect him and the state), crossed the finish line first. With the victory the 17-year-old runner became the state champion of 2015. Bent over with his hands on his knees before starting his cooldown walk, Zeke glanced at the competitors still running hard to the finish line. He noticed that one runner, about 25 meters out, was struggling beyond normal.

Zeke said, "I didn't know who he was or what school he was from, but his face was turning white, he was holding his chest, about to fall and looked awful." Zeke shouted for someone to help, but no one did. So Zeke rushed to the side of this runner, put his arm around him and walked with him for about 15 meters, then stepped aside to let him finish on his own. You'd think people would respond proudly to such a gesture from a 17-year-old competitor. Well, unfortunately, some didn't.

The assistant director of that state high school association stripped Zeke of his state championship medal, saying "that teen's act of sportsmanship violated the National Federation of State High School Association race rules." You read that right: sportsmanship "violated" race rules! Although the prep running community appealed the decision, the state association refused to reverse it. "Rules are rules," it declared. Well, suppose that struggling runner had collapsed and even died? What then?

Zeke said, "It was very disappointing. I did all that work during the summer for nothing." No, Zeke, it was not for nothing. You did what needed to be done, but there were unfair consequences.

Zeke, would you do it again? He was not hesitant in his answer: "Of course I'd do it again, because it was the right thing to do!" Thanks, Zeke!

Will you do what needs to be done because it's the right thing to do?

After further review …

"Fie, foh and fum, I smell the blood of a British man," is a line from Shakespeare's "King Lear," spoken by the character of Edgar. Many of us will recall a similar couplet used in the classic English fairy tale "Jack and the Beanstalk." That venerable rhyme came to mind again recently, when the U.S. Justice department—led by Attorney General Loretta Lynch—announced the arrest and indictment of 14 soccer and sports marketing executives. The "smell" was not of a single "British man" this time, but rather, the stench of corruption taking place at the highest levels of FIFA.

The 162-page document names nine FIFA (Federation Internationale de Football Association) members and five associated sports marketing officials. The indictment specifies that "… the defendants and their co-conspirators corrupted the enterprise by engaging in various criminal activities, including fraud, bribery, and money laundering, in pursuit of personal and political gain."

How much gain, you ask? How about an alleged $150 million in bribes and schemes linked to rights for tournaments in North and South America? Five of the seven arrested in Zurich were either FIFA vice presidents, executive committee members, or both. The indictment cites $10 million as having been wired to corrupt North American officials in exchange for voting for South Africa as the 2010 World Cup host. Also in question are the votes that placed the 2018 and 2022 World Cup events in Russia and Qatar, respectively.

FIFA president Joseph S, "Sepp" Blatter, the most prominent man in the world of "football" (as soccer is known globally) was elected to his fifth four-year by a vote of 133-72, just days after the arrests. "Definitely that is not me," said Blatter, concerning an unnamed top-level executive tied to the investigation. "I have no $10 million." As he has done in years past, Blatter shrugged off accusations of personal corruption and refused to resign, when the U.S. indictments were made public on May 27. On June 2, Blatter resigned, pending a FIFA special election.

Of great concern here are millions of kids around the world who start out just "kicking a can" in the street and alleys, dreaming of playing in the World Cup one day. They share those dreams with young American boys playing "touch" football in their own streets, dreaming of a chance to play in the NFL. And they share them with all the kids who shoot hoops nailed to garage doors, hoping to hit "nothing but net," like a Steph Curry 3-pointer (if the hoop has one).

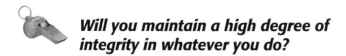

Will you maintain a high degree of integrity in whatever you do?

7 JUDGMENT

After further review …

It is disturbing to consider how much anger exists in our society, and how many people with failing self-control skills are walking among us, liable to erupt at any moment. Do television and the motion picture industry encourage the violence that has become so commonplace, with the steady stream of violent content that they produce? Does our society really want to allow, and can it endure, this behavior? The images of Sandy Hook, Columbine and other equally brutal random killings will remain with us for a lifetime.

Is the sports world culpable? Some sporting events are, by design as well as by nature, violent. Yet they do not have to be vicious. Our game of American football is currently under serious attack by those who decry its controlled violence, but it doesn't have to be, and it shouldn't be, provided we deal with this essential question: Are we raising a younger generation with the mindset to hate opponents? And does a "win-at-any-cost" attitude sap the character from the games we play?

Herm Edwards, former NFL player, head coach and current ESPN analyst, has been quoted as saying, "You play to win the game!" Having closely observed both his playing and coaching days, I can confirm that Edwards treats football as a game, but a game in which you give your best and honest effort every time, every play. Edwards never resorted to nor allowed his team the use of foul language or abhorrent behavior.

This brings us to a high school football game played between John Jay High School and Marble Falls High School, in San Antonio, Texas. Near the end of a recent game, two defensive players from John Jay targeted one of the officials. The first player violently and intentionally blindsided that official, hitting him in the back and knocking him down, after which the second player "speared" him as he lay helplessly on the ground. If you've seen the viral video, you probably couldn't believe your eyes either.

What in the world would cause such aggression toward an official? Well, it seems that a John Jay assistant coach was unhappy with the officiating and encouraged his players to get even, and thus that cowardly assault. (Two other John Jay players were ejected earlier in that game for unsportsmanlike acts, and the team ultimately lost 15-9.) Of course, you play to win the game, but losing is part of any game—as it is in life. Thus, the importance of a moral compass!

"Keep coming back and though the world may romp against your spine, let every game's end find you still on the battling line. For when the One Great Scorer comes to mark against your name He writes—not that you won or lost—but how you played the game!" Thank you, Grantland Rice.

 Will you treat your opponents and others with the same respect you desire?

December 15, 2014

After further review …

The headlines in an Oklahoma City newspaper read, "After Referees Blunder, Next Call is a Judge's." A district judge was scheduled to affirm or invalidate a high school's claim of an on-field official's call.* A high school in Oklahoma City is seeking to have the final 64 seconds of the second half replayed because of an admitted and crucial on-field mistake by the officiating crew.

At issue is whether the officials' mistake is correctable or whether human error is allowed to stand. The play in question was a foul called on one of the coaches, who was so excited that his team had scored a 58-yard touchdown to take a 25-20 lead over their rival opponent that he unintentionally impeded or bumped into the sideline official covering the play.

Since the coach had been warned earlier in that game for a similar infraction, a foul was called. Rules state that a 5-yard penalty is to be enforced on the try-for-point or the ensuing kickoff—with the touchdown counting. Instead, the officiating crew assessed a 5-yard penalty and disallowed the touchdown. By the way, the entire crew of officials must share in the responsibility for proper penalty enforcement.

A couple of questions come to mind: What if this same play and foul occurred in the first 64 seconds of the game and the same wrongful penalty was enforced? But the real question is: Should legal entities become involved in athletic contests?

Many argue that judgment calls should not be adjudicated other than by those supervisors responsible. Game officials' calls are reviewed by supervisors from the high school level to the professional level mostly with the intent to improve the officials' judgment. This "blunder," however, was not one of incorrect judgment, but an incorrect enforcement of the penalty. Are incorrect enforcements reviewable and corrected after a game?

One irate high school administrator said, "Adults in a split-second can negate months and years of hard work by kids who shouldn't be held accountable for these mistakes—especially in a situation when they can be corrected." Hmmmm.

*As this column went to press, word came that the judge disallowed the school's claim on the basis it was "unreasonable," arbitrary and without basis.

 Will you support the judge's decision?

After further review …

It was thrilling to see 23,239 San Diego Padre fans attend the ceremonies at Petco Park on June 26, 2014 to pay tribute to "Mr. Padre," Tony Gwynn, the Hall-of-Famer who played his entire 20-year career with the Padres. Oh, there wasn't a game being played and, no, Gwynn wasn't there. Gwynn had died of oral cancer 10 days earlier. Well, maybe he was there in spirit and hopefully, his spirit left a clear message.

His death is officially recorded as "salivary gland cancer." While there are no conclusive studies that compare chewing tobacco to mouth or throat cancer, Gwynn was "absolutely convinced" that "dipping" was the cause of his cancer. Near the end of his life he spoke of its dangers. Yet baseball players still dip in large numbers. In fact, a recent story on HBO's "Real Sports with Bryant Gumbel" program asserted that it is almost "expected" of young players entering professional baseball.

Many years ago Major League Baseball banned the smoking of cigarettes on the field. (Yes, players used to smoke on the field between innings and breaks in the action.) More recently MLB has asked its players and coaches to keep their dip—also called "chew," "snuff" and "chaw"—out of the sight of fans. Are you kidding me? Just observe the dugout behavior of any MLB team and you'll see the unsightliness of all that brown spittle.

So if smokeless tobacco is dangerous to a player's health and repugnant to a great many fans, why doesn't MLB ban it from the field? If you call the Major League Baseball Players Association you will likely get this answer: It's a civil liberties issue. That's the union saying MLB cannot dictate the personal habits of its players. About one-third of MLB players today dip, yet, the other two-thirds remain silent. Some suspect that the MLBPA would go along with a ban on smokeless tobacco, but will hold that "card" as a bargaining chip in further negotiations with MLB powerbrokers. Meanwhile, more will suffer with cancer and die as the bargaining chip remains.

Although minor leagues have banned smokeless tobacco, huge numbers of young players idolize MLB players as they watch games on television. Even with some major league stars issuing warnings about the dangers, those messages fall on deaf ears to the young idolizer, who believes that dipping is a part of baseball greatness.

Will you help young baseball players avoid the dangers of smokeless tobacco?

After further review …

When I was a kid, no one could keep me off the playground after school, or during weekends, holidays and vacations. No one? Well, maybe my mom, when it was time for dinner or my chores weren't done. I always had a ball, glove, bat and the necessary equipment, thanks to dad being a playground director. As the seasons changed, so would my chosen sport, from football to basketball to baseball.

That doesn't seem to be the case in today's youth sports. Parents and coaches steer kids toward hopeful success in a single sport, often with the eventual goal of securing a college scholarship and even at the chance to play at the professional level. At very young ages, kids are competing year-round in select "club" organizations, devoted to one sport.

As we begin this year's baseball season, the name Tommy John surfaces. John was a left-handed Major League Baseball pitcher who played 26 seasons for six teams (one team twice). He is best known as the namesake for the "Tommy John Surgery," which occurred in the middle of his career (1974) when he was pitching for the Los Angeles Dodgers. John, 13-3 at that point in the season, had damaged his ulnar collateral ligament. The probable cause of his injury was due to his sinkerball pitch, virtually impossible to hit. It was thought that he would never pitch again. However, he rehabbed the elbow, skipping the 1975 season, and returned to pitch 13 more seasons.

The successful surgery was good news/bad news for baseball as major league elbows today are wearing out at record rates. Already this season two players have opted to have that surgery.

"There is a real sense of urgency to understand the entire TJ surgery now," said Stan Conte, the Dodgers' vice president of medical services. Over the past three years there has been an average of 28 TJ surgeries in Major League Baseball, more than double the rate of the years 2000-10.

What is of bigger concern is that some teenage prospects are electing to have the TJ surgery. The American Sports Medicine Institute said that these injuries begin when these kids are adolescent amateurs. Research points to overuse, poor pitching mechanics and poor physical fitness. While prematurely throwing curveballs is often a trigger, the ASMI's research cites insufficient physical development, neuromuscular control and overuse due to improper coaching as underlying causes.

Will you observe closely how your youngsters develop as balanced and healthy athletes?

After further review …

There is currently much dialogue about concussions in contact sports. The National Football League has been a leader in developing and enforcing what is termed "concussion protocol."

"Concussion is an important injury for the professional player, and the diagnosis, prevention, and management of concussion is important to the NFL, its players and member Clubs (read: teams) and the NFL Players Association. The NFL's Head, Neck, and Spine Committee has developed a comprehensive set of protocols with regard to the diagnosis and management of concussions in NFL players."

Every parent should be knowledgeable about, or at least aware, of the types of injuries that may occur due to such simple and normal risks when youngsters fall off their bikes or skateboards, even while wearing protective head gear. Such head gear may prevent cuts and bruises, but not necessarily concussions. NFL players wear technically advanced helmets, yet concussions—the result of the brain colliding with the interior of the skull—occur with some frequency. The symptoms can be difficult to observe externally and further masked by a kid insisting he's OK in order to continue playing. This topic will not, and should not, go away. Awareness is key!

Of concern here is the 2015 Women's World Cup soccer tournament, and the extensive use of "headers," the soccer term for airborne balls redirected by a leaping player's head. Almost every player does it, and one can imagine the impact of a 1-pound leather ball traveling at speeds of 30 to 60 mph. Every time I saw it happen, the word "concussion" flashed through my mind. There's a growing concern expressed by medical experts and soccer legends that this sport needs to "use its head" when it comes to player safety.

Recently a group of California parents filed a class-action suit that would limit how many times children under 17 can "head" the ball. As if there were a "safe" number. You kiddin' me? How about none? "Why are we turning our kids' heads into battering rams?" said the executive director of the Sports Legacy Institute.

Scientists say repeated blows to the head, whether from collisions with other players or simply heading the ball, can lead to memory loss, confusion, aggression or chronic traumatic encephalopathy (CTE).

Yes, eliminating headers from the game of soccer will change its nature, and maybe rightly so. New rules in football have changed the game—for the better. Basketball, especially the NBA, needs to follow suit.

 Will you be able to convince others that safety rules need to come first?

After further review …

Remember the old saw, "Careful what you ask for?" It's always a good reminder when we become satisfied or satiated with our present conditions. Sports fans certainly must enjoy this time of year! Wherever you live in the U.S.—or in the entire world, for that matter—there's a game or match being played in your area. If not, your warm, comfy easy chair and a TV remote will fly you into the stadium on time.

With a smartphone or smartwatch, the game will follow you wherever you go. Here's an exhausting schedule (not in any particular order) to which you can log in:

The NFL, with its 32 teams, has now completed two-thirds of its regular-season schedule. This 2015 season began with the Hall of Fame game held in Canton, Ohio, in August, in conjunction with the HoF induction ceremonies. The final game—Super Bowl 50 (a variance from the Roman numerals previously used to identify the Super Bowl, which, by the way, was originally not called the Super Bowl) will be played in Santa Clara on Feb. 7, 2016.

The NBA, with 30 clubs, began its season in October and will end with its championship games on or about the middle of June 2016. In the middle of that 82-game schedule is the 65th NBA All-Star game, to be held (is your passport valid?) at the Air Canada Centre in Toronto, Ontario (home of the Raptors) on Feb. 14, 2016. It's a three-day event! Oops, maybe you're already booked, since that's Valentine's Day weekend!

The NHL, 32 teams strong, began its schedule Oct. 7 and will close its 82-game season with the commencement of the 98th Stanley Cup playoffs on April 11. Last year's Stanley Cup contender was the Tampa Bay Lightning. Many have taken note of the irony inherent in a team of ice skating champions from the tropics. Picking up where the Jamaican bobsledders left off, perhaps?

The NASCAR Sprint Cup series, with up to five events every month for almost the entire year, should satisfy those who follow that sport. Some critics say that since the machine does all the work, it's a misnomer to use the term "sport" in comparison with athletes performing on the field or court. But at 170 mph, and in close proximity to your competitors (even closer than fellow commuters on the 405 in L.A.!), it takes great physical skill not to end up on the wall.

And if all that isn't enough, the NCAA began its 2015-16 basketball schedule at midnight in early November, and will conclude its annual "March Madness" with the Final Four championship game on April 4, 2016 in Houston, Texas.

Will you log in about your favorite sport and whether you like watching in person or TV?

After further review …

Coach Don Shula and Dr. Ken Blanchard, two close friends and colleagues, co-authored a book titled "Everyone's A Coach." The book's major point of emphasis is that "you can inspire anyone to be a winner." It stresses that winning is not dependent upon trick plays, formations or systems, but instead, as Shula points out "comes down to a matter of motivating people to work hard and prepare to play as a team."

That's a big truth stated by one of its indisputable masters. Shula has won more NFL games as a coach than anyone in history! His 347 victories while coaching the Baltimore Colts and Miami Dolphins during his 33 years as a head coach will never be surpassed. Passing and rushing records will fall, touchdown marks have a shelf-life, but Shula's lifetime wins will never be exceeded. If that should happen, please contact me and I'll personally buy you the finest steak dinner at one of Shula's Steak Houses, which is redundant.

Blanchard is a professional speaking colleague who has written 63 (and counting) books on leadership and considered a mastermind in that industry. His wildly successful "The One Minute Manager" has sold 13 million copies and is still considered (written in 1981) a benchmark in the business world.

All that said, it is ironic to observe the gazillion folks who may believe that investing in a book will imbue them with the brilliance that inspired it. That was not Shula's or Blanchard's intent. The world these days seems to be full of coaches, each one better than whomever he or she is criticizing. Most have never been in the position of a coach, yet appear to possess the certain knowledge of who to play, which plays to run, and how to correct any problems that arise. The media helps stimulate this opinionated speculation, but I guess that's what they get paid for.

When Kansas City Royals manager Ned Yost was told of a fan's harsh criticism, he responded that he doesn't read newspapers or watch television during the season. Yost said when the MLB season is over he loves to go hunting with his bow and arrow. "Bow and arrow? Why don't you use a gun?" came the question. The second-guessing never stops! We need to remember that the term "fan" is short for "fanatic." Ya gotta love 'em!

Will you be respectful of another's decision without being judgmental?

After further review …

Stop the world—I wanna get off is a theme often heard when someone is frustrated with life, or happenings therein.

One of the ardent readers of On the TUNNEYSIDE of Sports recently wrote regarding the "shocking" story about the players on the Virginia State University football team who reportedly beat up the quarterback of the Winston-Salem State team. No, this was not during the game, but at a luncheon the day before their scheduled league championship game. Huh?

The two schools were to play for the CIAA (Central Intercollegiate Athletic Association) championship the following day. The CIAA was formed in 1912 and comprises historically of black colleges ranging from Pennsylvania to North Carolina.

At the pre-game luncheon the Winston-Salem quarterback was in the men's room when several of the Virginia State players allegedly approached him and "punched, stomped and kicked him several times." My reader wrote, "What? Are you kidding me?" followed by the "Stop-the-world" statement.

That championship game was cancelled and the CIAA authorized its commissioner to conduct an investigation. One Virginia State player has been charged with a "misdemeanor assault." While accounts from the two schools differ, the result of the unfortunate event is clear: the championship game was cancelled. Winston-Salem was allowed to play Slippery Rock in the Division II playoffs and the Virginia State players were left on the sidelines during post-season play. Some finger pointing has blamed the Virginia State University administration for not having better supervision of its players.

It is certainly appropriate to have supervision of players, but these are university-level athletes. Do they need the same supervision necessary for players at the high school level? I mean, these are not gang-banger type athletes. Do they need that close observance?

What captured the attention of this reader was the abhorrent behavior of athletes at the college level; thus, his euphemistic departure statement. Should we hold athletes to a higher level? We say, "Yes!"

 Will you follow simple rules of civility in your life situations?

December 16, 2013

After further review …

A family friend, who teaches fourth graders in our community, recently asked her twenty-five students 'What would you like to be when you grow up?' She said the question was designed to help students in the class get to know each other better. Further, she asked each student to stand in giving their response. While they were asked to stand, you had better sit down in reading their answers.

Most of them said "Famous" or "Rock Star" or "Celebrity" or "NBA Star" (not simply player, but "star") Another student said "A millionaire" and when asked why, replied "'Cause a millionaire doesn't have to work, he can just do whatever he wants all day." The composition of this class is broad in its ethnicity with representative kids from Caucasian, African-American, Asian, and Middle Eastern backgrounds. The stereotypical American middle class of previous generations, full of candidates for the "white collar" jobs their educations were geared to, are not so evident in this group. So be it; it's a different world with different priorities that we inhabit now.

But some things remain the same. Did you know what you wanted to be as an adult when you were in the fourth grade? The world of dreams and the world of work do not always line up neatly with each other. Can one fault these nine-year olds for their answers in 2013, when they are bombarded by television and the internet content that glamorizes wealth and privilege and ease?

The signing of free-agent baseball player Robinson Cano by the Seattle Mariners made headlines in most of the country's major newspapers this week. It took a 10-year, $240 million contract to lure him away from the perennially well-to-do Yankees. Cano is a second baseman. He has three or four at-bats per game and fields a similar number of ground balls. Next season, he will make approximately $150,000 per game.

The Dominican Cano's namesake Jackie Robinson never had a 10-year contract and probably never made $150,000 in his entire 10-year MLB career.

Any wonder why today's kids are so seduced by the big money and all the attention it attracts? Kobe Bryant: two years, $24 million. Bartolo Colon: two years, $20 million. The cost of four MLB free agents in 2013 ($538,000,000) exceeds the anticipated costs ($425,000,000) of a 2016 mission to Mars.

Is this what the "American Dream" has become? Is this what this millennium generation of kids expects as their due? What's it all about Alfie?

 Will you log in your thoughts about how our young people can build a more realistic future?

After further review …

The NCAA Division I Men's Basketball tournament brackets were announced Sunday, and we hope your T*E*A*M was among them. If not, you may wonder why, since so many "at-large" teams are now invited to the dance—some with less than-glamorous playing records.

We will eventually arrive at the Final Four in early April, but the road there—to the delight of millions of the fervent—travels through March Madness.

This week's theme is "6 on a Side," suggested by the fact that so many of the NCAA coaches occupy court space during games, either exhorting their players or yelling at the officials for their "dreadful" officiating. The NCAA has a rule against being on the court, so why do so many coaches break it?

One answer may be that team benches are so close to the boundary lines that when a coach gets up out of his seat, he's practically on the floor.

Having had the privilege of playing, coaching and officiating basketball for over three decades, I can understand a coach's frustrations. College basketball has changed significantly along with the growth of its players.

Today's game is played largely "above the rim," which is inherently more difficult to officiate. (I found my coaching experience helpful to my officiating perspective, but those worlds don't intersect much anymore.)

A noted coach recently said "basketball is an emotional game, and others are asking you to be unemotional." No coach, we're not.

But we are asking that you exercise enough self-control to stay off the court. The sanctity of basketball depends on a conduct framework for the game that allows coaches to voice their displeasure with a call (or no-call), as long as they do it with civility—hmm, there's that word again.

Game officials are more than ever under the constant scrutiny of fans through the myriad eyes of personal devices that see everything and communicate instantly. Indeed, viewers now see more of the intricacies of the game than ever before.

Today's coach is typically a sophisticated analyst of all that information and data. Many coaches have said "I do my coaching before the game, and with a proper game plan, I can sit down and enjoy my players and the game better."

 Will you log in with your opinion about the behavior of today's college coaches?

After further review …

One of the reasons many people—young and old alike—admire the sports world is that it runs by a set of clear rules. Players just can't appear on the field or court and express any behavioral whim that they feel. Although it might be wished that society's rules and norms were more uniformly observed, there is a compensatory civility and a dedication to common sense built right into sports. Officials are in place to penalize or prevent any disregard of the set rules. Thus the integrity of the games is insured.

Early in Major League Baseball's 2014 season we've seen some extravagant challenges to the rules for the sake of an advantage. One took place in a recent game between the New York Yankees and the Boston Red Sox. MLB Rule 8.02(a) (2-6) Page 75 states "the pitcher shall not apply a foreign substance of any kind to the ball." I wonder what part of that rule Yankees pitcher Michael Pineda didn't understand?

Pineda had a patch of pine tar (a woolly mammoth could have disappeared in) under his right ear, and it earned him a 10-day suspension. Maybe Pineda just didn't understand the importance of discretion. His own team had earlier warned him that opponents were sure to notice his free use of the sticky stuff if he didn't lighten up. (Pine tar enhances fingertip grip, and therefore spin, for pitchers relying on sinking or breaking balls.)

Pineda was sheepishly reported by Red Sox manager John Farrell, who complained to plate umpire Gerry Davis during the second inning of that game. After an almost comical, 360-degree exam of Pineda by Davis, the Yankees pitcher was ejected—embarrassing for all concerned. The rule is routinely broken but even so, a secondary unofficial rule comes into play: don't be brazen enough to get caught. It's a bizarre rule that only baseball folks can understand.

Who really knows what constitutes cheating anymore? Pitchers have substances under their sleeves or in their gloves. Catchers hide pine tar on their shin guards, then rub some on the ball before returning it to the pitcher. It seems that the number one defense is to proclaim that "everybody does it." Huh?

 Will you log in on how bizarre rules ought to be enforced?

After further review …

Shortly after the buzzer sounded in game 6 of the NBA Western Conference finals, the "Heat" was on. After eliminating the Oklahoma City Thunder, the San Antonio Spurs turned their attention to the NBA Finals and the prospect of revenge against the Miami Heat. Before the first tip-off, the battle of words intensified.

"It's unbelievable that we have regained focus after that devastating loss that we had last year, but we're back and we're excited about it. We've got four more to win. We'll do it this time," proclaimed veteran Spurs forward Tim Duncan, immediately after the game with sweat dripping by the quart. Doesn't sound too obnoxious, does it? Seemed more like a self-confident player and a self-confident team announcing its intentions. (By the way, of all the NBA teams these two best exemplify the team rather than the "It's-all-about-me" game).

Forward LeBron James, Duncan's All-Pro counterpart on the Heat, took up the gauntlet with his response: "They don't like us. They don't. I can sense it from Timmy's comments over the last couple days." Timmy? Hmm. Sounds like a couple of kids on the playground. James was from St.Vincent-St.Mary's Catholic High School in Akron, and Duncan formerly of St. Dunstan's Episcopal High School of St.Croix, U.S. Virgin Island. The religious training was inconspicuous in their crossfire. Perhaps a better analysis of their comments might be: It's just all hype.

Anyway, Duncan's assertion seemed to be to spirit-on his teammates, which they did in game 1 winning, 110-95. But did the Spurs have to resort to turning-off the air conditioning at the AT&T Center? (Note: Game 2 was played after this went to press.)

While it is recognized that the media plays an important part in today's pro sports market, it is hoped that this sort of "jawing" is not a part of our youth sports. Teams win on the field and court, not in the press.

 *Will you watch sporting events to see which team performs better?*

After further review …

It was thrilling to see the 23,239 fans attend the ceremonies at Petco Park, the home of the San Diego Padres, one day recently. Oh, there wasn't a ballgame. But fans sat for three hours to say farewell to "Mr. Padre" Tony Gwynn, who died of oral cancer June 16.

The tributes flowed, along with tears, from Hall of Famers, current and retired players, coaches and former teammates—the variety was overwhelming. Their words were not about Gwynn's .338 lifetime batting average or his 3,121 hits or five Gold Glove awards, or even those eight batting titles. No, they were more about the spirit of Anthony Keith Gwynn.

There was a certain irony in his Gold Glove awards. When Gwynn began his major league career he was not a good fielder, he had a wobbly gait and his arm strength was mediocre. But he seemed to heed his own guidance, his words set in stone outside Petco Park: "If you work hard, good things will happen."

Perhaps the most significant fact is that he remained a Padre throughout his 20-year career, playing in 2,440 games. He could have used free agency to find another team that might have paid him more money, but he didn't (are you listening, LeBron?). When Gwynn retired in 2001, he could have gone into broadcasting. His intelligence and baseball knowledge certainly would have commanded a high-level salary. But he didn't.

Instead, Gwynn became the head baseball coach at San Diego State, his alma mater. During his 12 years with the Aztecs, he gave back to baseball some of what he felt he owed—expert instruction, autographs, along with his signature smile for the lines of players and fans alike waiting to share a little time with Mr. Padre. He left behind many valuable lessons.

Not least was the one that figured in his fate. Tony Gwynn was a longtime user of smokeless tobacco, commonly referred to as "snuff." Snuff and chewing tobacco are still used at most levels of baseball. Gwynn spoke of its dangers near the end of his life. While not illegal, Major League Baseball has asked its players and coaches to keep it out of sight of young fans.

 Will you learn from the lessons left by Mr. Padre?

October 6, 2014

After further review …

"The Captain has left the building!" Or more accurately, "the field." Or perhaps you hear the voice of legendary New York Yankee announcer Bob Sheppard, annunciating in his distinguished tone, "Numbah 2, Derek Jee-tah numbah 2." After 20 years as the Yankee shortstop, Jeter has retired and will proudly walk away.

This tribute to "numbah 2" is not because he has the most hits ever for a Yankee, and it's not because in his last at-bats in the bottom of the ninth he drove in the winning run to beat the Orioles 6-5 with a "walk-off" (dislike that term) single. No, this is about Jeter—the role model!

It's a time-honored compliment to say of someone that "if you looked up the word (quality "x") in the dictionary you'd see so-and-so's picture." It certainly holds true for Jeter. Plug in respect, or better yet re2pect, for quality "x" and you're likely to find a picture of Derek Jeter in his legendary No. 2 Yankee uniform. He certainly epitomizes the definition of that word, eliciting "high or special regard" from a couple of generations of Yankee fans.

As Paul Anka wrote and Frank Sinatra sang: "For what is a man, what has he got? If not himself, then he has naught." Jeter had always been Jeter! In his words he "worked hard every day to do my job (as a Yankee shortstop) to the standard I expect of myself." He remained a single man, because "I knew I couldn't give what was needed or expected of me and do justice to being a husband and father."

"Don't disappoint yourself" is the axiom Dot and Charles Jeter taught their son. Dot, a Caucasian, and Charles, an African-American, knew what a challenge living up to those words could pose. They raised Derek in an earlier era, when children of racially mixed-marriages were more likely to encounter bigotry, and standing up for oneself took dignity and courage. Derek says he heard an occasional derogatory remark, yet never became bitter or allowed those remarks to define his character. "Respect people like you want to be respected," Charles would say.

It would be hard to find someone Derek ever snubbed or failed to treat with the utmost respect. That's why it's called RE2PECT!

 Will you adapt No. 2's philosophy and respect others as you want to be respected?

8 MENTORING

iStock/Thinkstock

After further review …

Speaking to corporations, associations, and businesses of all types, my goal is to remind the audience to "celebrate their successes." NFL players do that when they cross the goal line, (though many may take it to extremes). So with celebration in mind, I write my 500th consecutive column/blog and remind myself how much I enjoy creating them, but even more, how grateful I am to each of you who read them. Every day I hear from people how much they appreciate these essays.

The impetus for the column came, I guess, when I was identifying my life's ambition, which occurred when I was about 12. That's when I knew I wanted to be a coach. Writing was the furthest thing on my agenda. Coaching sports was my goal and I pursued that. As I moved into school administration (which led to becoming a district superintendent), I segued into professional speaking as well. My coaching emphasis became less about X's and O's and more about helping people realize their potential.

During my X's and O's career I would try to engage my players mentally prior to workouts and games. To me, the preparation of the mind preceded the physical work. I would hang signs on the classroom wall delivering the message that "all action begins with thought."

A history lesson taught me that the word "coach" was first used in England in the 1500s. A coach was (and still is) a horse-drawn carriage used to transport people from where they are to where they want or need to be. That concept has been at the heart of the column. Perhaps one or more of the following aphorisms will help inspire you:

- People need to be reminded more than they need to be informed.
- Never forget what you receive, but forget what you gave.
- I can't do all the world needs, but the world needs all I can do.
- Forget what hurt you, but never forget what it taught you.
- People are like steel. When they lose their temper, they lose their worth.
- Experience is the ability to recognize a mistake, when you make it again.
- It's not how old you are, but how you are old.
- Confidence is when you are down two scores in the fourth quarter and still believe you can win.
- Best words of encouragement a parent can say: "I really enjoy watching you play."

Will you walk your talk with expressions that may help you live a better life?

After further review …

Once upon a time, there was a very shy young lad, shy to the point of being timid. His fear of failing affected many areas of his life. His self-esteem was below the level of his classmates. His marks in elementary school were passing, but he felt he wasn't as smart as the others. He had friends, but was not outgoing.

Although athletically inclined, sports were not his focus. He leaned toward baseball, but when he was failing and wanted to quit, the encouragement of his father prevented it. His dad was partial to golf and provided clubs for his son at an early age. Golf is a difficult game at best; failing is almost built into the sport. The boy wanted to quit, and the patience of his parents was tested, but they continued bringing him to the golf course.

At about age 7, he joined the AT&T Pebble Beach Junior Golf Association and continued to improve, but losing was still his nemesis. Joining some junior golf buddies, he began to compete in some tournaments. Playing in those events became fun and somehow made it easier to fail, when that happened—and it did.

One of the biggest impacts was the improvement in his attitude, which helped build his confidence. He continued to overcome his fear of failure. In one of those junior golf tournaments, he hit his drive out of bounds—three holes in a row! In the past he would have walked off the course. Not that day, and although his ego was bruised, he finished the game with a good attitude, saying to himself, "Just one of those days …"

He gives credit to his dramatic change in attitude to the game of golf and the opportunity to learn it through the Junior Golf Association. His life as a student changed as well. He is graduating from high school this year with a GPA of 4.28 to go along with his .8 golf handicap. He still doesn't like to fail, but has come to realize the value of failing helped him grow as a person. He calls it "learning to fail forward" and has moved from a passive spectator to an active participant. The importance of the AT&T Pebble Beach Junior Golf program is second to none in helping young people become confident and positive adults.

 Will you support junior golf so that other youngsters might grow as this young man did?

After further review …

Are we experiencing a dearth of role models today? How vital are they in the interplay between the world of sports and society? Can we build a nation's character without benefit of strong, positive examples to follow? What are the criteria for their selection?

In my book "Impartial Judgment," I made this statement: "We all need mentors and I had the best." I was referring first to my father, whose behavior and achievements I have always sought to emulate.

This responsibility is a natural one for parents to assume and many, like my dad, meet it willingly and selflessly. But many don't or are not available, resulting in a vacuum of guidance for too many young people. When this occurs, alternative role models are called for, and they need not be from the same family, ethnicity, or culture. What matters is personal integrity, and dedication to the work required for success in all of life's pursuits. I was fortunate to have the advice of many others that crossed my path.

When I met Jack Roosevelt Robinson ("Jackie" #42) at the age of 9, was it acceptable for me to model the behavior of a man I so admired? Of course it was! A book titled, "Reach," now on the market and edited by my friend the former NAACP President Ben Jealous, contains real-life stories about black men both famous and not-so-famous who overcame very arduous backgrounds to succeed in today's world. Is this book intended solely for black men? Absolutely not! Or men only? Again, no! The path to success follows a universal map.

Behavior is the model, not ethnicity or gender. One doesn't have to be an Andrew Luck, Derek Jeter or Jimmy Rollins, or even in sports, to be admired. Rollins, "J-Roll" as he is called, now the Los Angeles Dodgers shortstop, was the 2014 Roberto Clemente Award recipient along with Chicago White Sox shortstop Paul Konerko. Rollins is black, Konerko is white, and Clemente was Puerto Rican. The award, shared last year for the first time, is given annually to a major league baseball player for his exemplary sportsmanship on the field and his community involvement off the diamond.

 Will you select your role models with no regard for their gender or ethnicity, but for the quality of their behavior?

February 15, 2015

After further review …

"Catch people doing something right" is one of the messages I use with organizations interested in building a better team. As a parent, teacher, coach, school administrator and NFL referee, I learned that the best way to help others achieve is to build their confidence. As an example, if you are witnessing your youngster lacking confidence in his or her sport, you might offer encouragement by saying, "I really enjoy watching you play."

Everyone wants to do their best. No one intentionally performs badly. Yet, when we don't measure up to our (or others') expectations, we need helpful guidance and encouragement to improve. Super Bowl XLIX was a good example of teams giving their best. Although the final moments of the game resulted in criticism of one coach and team, no one involved in real-time game decisions intentionally makes the wrong call. We'll let fans take it from here.

Let's remember there are three teams in any football game. Mistakes made by any one of those three can affect the outcome. The NFL officiating crew in Super Bowl XLIX headed, by referee Bill Vinovich, performed to the highest expected standards. The two teams decided that game, and that's the way all games are expected to be played.

It is often said that the best-officiated games are those in which the officials were "hardly noticed." When the game is over the only question concerning the officiating should be, "Who were those guys?" Minimally noticed, but having impact. When the officials do their job as expected, their impact is that the integrity of the game is held to its highest standard.

Every NFL crew strives to perform at its very best level, every week. NFL officials recognize that the "stars" of the game are the players and coaches. They're the ones the fans come to see. However, it's important to note that the game of football (or any athletic contest) could not function without proper game control. That's what we saw in the Super Bowl, and Vinovich's crew can't escape this positive assessment.

 Will you strive to help others improve by "catching them doing something right?"

After further review …

Today, we honor the work of Martin Luther King Jr. His famous "I have a dream" speech of some 52 years ago is still alive, but wanting. We still want equality for all; yet a dream is only that until we spur it into action. The society Dr. King dreamed of is a work in progress. The same may be said for the sports world.

"I have a dream" that every athlete treats the opportunity to participate in sports as a privilege, with respect for one's opponents being one of its defining characteristics. While rule-makers attempt to eliminate "trash talking" through punishment of offenders, it is well known that a penalty has only a Band-Aid effect. The first step in eliminating poor behavior is role modeling that begins at home, followed with reinforcement from teachers and coaches.

Yes, it does take courage for parents, teachers and everyone involved in the education of youth to "step up" with verbal guidance and correction in order to provide a proper path. Setting a positive example is frequently the most effective tool. Young people today are exposed to many diverse types of behavior: they are often confused about which direction to take. Yet, almost any 5-year-old inherently knows right from wrong. If those lessons learned at home reinforce that instinctive sense of right or wrong, a child is off to a healthy start.

Having recently watched more than three dozen football bowl or playoff games, it was easy to observe those coaches who, although desperately trying to win, showed behavior in concert with acceptable standards. Then, too, there were others who ignored egregious behavior by focusing on winning rather than stepping up to correct an unwanted act.

But what method of improvement is best? Let's start with the negative. When performance is less than expected, it does little good to threaten "If your performance doesn't improve, you will be fired!" In order for that person to improve, specific, attainable methods must be shown that the performer can learn and repeat. As a sports example, it doesn't do much good to say, "Don't fumble the football!" The player already knows that. What he needs to know are the techniques that he can apply to prevent the fumble.

 Will you help others improve their performance by citing specific, attainable behaviors?

After further review …

"Stork" was the nickname we labeled him in our early days on the playground. Those early days of friendship eventually numbered 76 years until recently, when he was called to the Lord. He is there now, I'm sure, with his wife and one of his sons. His given name was William Robert Boyd, and he generally answered to Bob, except for those who knew him as Stork. That nickname was appropriate; as a kid he was taller, skinny and ganglier than the rest of us.

Bob and I grew up together on the Washington Grammar School playground in San Gabriel. I lived just nine houses from that school. Bob lived a half-mile away. He was 8 and I was 9 when we first met. While there were several of us who played on those school grounds (our "sandlot") after school, weekends and holidays, Bob and I connected for a lifetime.

We always had the right-shaped ball, and whatever equipment we needed, since my dad was the playground director for the city of Alhambra. We played everything: two-hand touch football on a dirt playground; netless basketball on asphalt, and over-the-line softball on a roughly-constructed diamond.

We attended Alhambra High School, playing basketball and baseball there—he was the starting center on our basketball team, and I was the starting bench-warmer. Bob was 6-foot-5 in the ninth grade (he was nearly that tall when he was 8). He couldn't have weighed more than 150 pounds then—thus the Stork moniker. Bob's junior (my senior) year, our basketball team tied for the league championship, but lost in the CIF playoffs.

Bob was an All-American selection playing at the University of Southern California, and then became a high school and college basketball coach. Thirteen of his coaching years were spent at his alma mater, where he sent several players to the NBA. Indeed, hundreds of players under his tutelage have gone on to success in many different life pursuits.

This is being written as a tribute to him in respect for what he did for so many young men—not just with their athletic training, but for what he taught them about living a good life and helping others. They miss him and so do I.

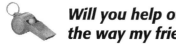 ***Will you help others be better people the way my friend Stork did?***

After further review …

Bullying: Coercion by superior strength or intimidation. It's an ugly definition, no matter how you phrase it, and this domination of the weaker by the stronger has been around far too long. This topic is a matter of great concern in current society—parents and guardians themselves are hyper-aware of its negative effects, and protective of their children. But parents themselves can fall prey to this deep-seated behavior, slipping into that coercive mode to get their own children to obey. Is it necessary? Oftentimes, it's not even recognized for what it is.

In our sports world many coaches, regrettably, resort to such methods, all in the name of motivation. Some coaches yell, scream, cuss and use derogatory names, thinking that their verbal abuse will bring intensity to their team. Sports reflect the culture in that regard; coaches who resort to intimidation more than likely were hollered at when they played. And parents quite often raise their children according to the examples set during their own upbringing. The concern is that some previously accepted methods may not be appropriate today.

Motivation is not a simple formula; many approaches are successful. But the most lasting and effective methods involve positive reinforcement. In my book, "It's the Will, Not the Skill," we discuss how former NFL head coach Herm Edwards (New York Jets, 2001-05, and Kansas Chiefs, 2006-09) now an analyst at ESPN, always told his players they were "born winners" and "are winners now," not that they will be, but now! Players must think of themselves as winners!

No one wins every time or at everything. Losses—or setbacks, if you will—are all part of being a winner. As many have said, it's not getting knocked down that counts, it's the will to get back up that matters. It is interesting to note that when one is winning and one's confidence is stout, the necessity of encouragement diminishes. However, having said that, the coach is needed to ensure that complacency does not occur.

Building a culture of self-confidence is not easy, but the persistence of the mentor, be it coach, parent or teacher, is paramount. Young people model behavior. Examples set by those in a leadership position are repeated for better or worse. Do we have a duty to strive for the "better" example? You bet we do!

Will you adopt the "Edwards Code" of modeling a positive, winning attitude?

After further review …

During a recent conversation I had with the executive director of the AT&T Pebble Beach Junior Golf Association, she was discussing the nine core values their junior golfers (ages 7-17) can learn from the great game of golf and further, put into practice in their daily lives. These were: respect, honesty, integrity, sportsmanship, confidence, responsibility, perseverance, courtesy and judgment. She said she was proud to be part of such a program.

The AT&T Pebble Beach Junior Golf Association is 25-years-young and preceded, maybe even gave impetus to, the nationwide First Tee movement. This junior golf program has 60 golf professionals on the Monterey Peninsula providing lessons, clinics, tournaments and scholarships for some 1,300 junior golfers.

The cost to these youths is an annual fee of $25. Golf clubs, hats and balls are provided free for any financially-challenged players. Tournament competition occurs within five age divisions (platinum, gold, silver, bronze and copper).

She was effusive in describing how remarkable the character of these youngsters is. Then she related a story about a young golfer who had finished a tournament third in his division. When he returned home he held his medallion up disgustedly and said to his father "Look, all I got was this dumb medal." It may be an isolated case, but how could any kid be ungrateful for finishing third? Is first place the only reward? Surely, there is a lesson to be learned here.

I wondered how that father responded. The opportunity to help an unhappy golfer overcome his disappointment could be crucial to the boy's future, since dealing with unfulfilled expectations will always be part of his live. As the ancient Greek philosopher Epicurus said, "It's not what happens to you, but how you react to it that matters." Now, this young man probably couldn't care less about Epicurus, but those nine core values can certainly help him. There are many ways a parent, coach, or teacher can be of positive benefit in these situations.

Oh, by the way, that executive director mentioned above is Linda Tunney, my wife, who for 18 years has been in charge of this valuable program. The Junior Golf Associations does so much for these kids, not the least of which is introducing them to those nine core values. Linda was recently inducted into the PGA Hall of Fame, Monterey Bay Chapter, for her service to golf and to young people. Way to go, Hon!

 Will your service to others be of Hall of Fame caliber?

After further review …

In his "Hierarchy of Needs" theory, the influential psychologist Abraham Maslow lists belonging as an important element in successful human development. Duty to family can provide that. Growing up with parents who were role models and mentors, my siblings and I were fortunate. We didn't choose our parents, but we respected their duty to us and never wanted to commit an act that would embarrass them. The love and feeling of belonging.

When we read or hear of some athletes whose behavior is less than honorable, even to the point of felony arrests, we have to wonder if, as children they were loved and felt like they belonged. DeSean Jackson and Richard Sherman—elite professional athletes—are currently in the news, due to the influence of alleged gang relationships in the past. They are cited here not to cast aspersions, but simply to examine how we strive for belonging, and how those choices may affect us.

Sherman, a Stanford graduate and now a cornerback for the Super Bowl XVLII champion Seattle Seahawks, was born and raised in Compton, an area well known for its gang turf battles. Jackson, a standout receiver both in college (Cal) and the NFL (Philadelphia Eagles), was raised by Gayle and Bill Jackson in Long Beach. Bill coached both athletes in youth leagues, and their relationship has continued through the years; both describe themselves as proud citizens of their challenged communities.

The Eagles recently released Jackson, citing "gang ties" in the announcement. (Note: Jackson was quickly signed by the Washington Redskins). Sherman and Jackson have each earned a reputation for "flamboyant" on-field behaviors, yet both have the potential to be positive NFL role models. Sherman, for example, was salutatorian of his high school senior class in Compton. Can we sense the need to "belong" here?

While going to college and playing in the NFL creates a natural distance, Sherman defends Jackson's ties: "the men with DeSean in the (recent) social pictures and police reports weren't his closest friends in childhood, but when his father died in 2009, few people were there for him. When a tragic event like that happens, the people who are around are the people who are around, and they were there for him."

Having spent my early teaching and coaching career (13 years) in an East Los Angeles high school with five active gangs in the community, I saw clearly that young boys and girls found love and belonging in a gang environment. Negativism became their family and way of life. We must help those so influenced to show them a better way.

 Will you offer your love to those who are trying to overcome negative environments? Will you help them feel like they belong?

After further review …

The Positive Coaching Alliance (www.positivecoach.org) is more than 15 years old and growing rapidly. Founded by Jim Thompson, the PCA's goal is to help develop "better athletes, better people." The alliance partners with more than 2,000 schools and youth sports organizations nationwide impacting more than 5 million youths to date.

It accomplishes this with workshops and courses throughout the country. The intent is to help coaches, parents and competitors teach and practice life lessons through sports. My columns/blogs are similar in design. It is the belief here there is no better way for people to work together than through positive examples learned from the sports fields and courts. The PCA board of advisers is comprised of an impressive array of coaches and athletes throughout the country who stress by their actions as well as by their words how character can be developed.

The PCA recently assembled a panel (at which I was privileged to attend) that emphasized the importance of coaching athletes from the inside out. The panel was composed of Steve Young, former San Francisco 49ers quarterback; David Shaw, Stanford head football coach; and Lindsey Gottlieb, women's basketball coach at Cal.

Young emphasized how the character and integrity of his 49ers coach, the late Bill Walsh, was important in helping him. Shaw mentioned that Andrew Luck, whom he coached, was such a role model that Luck's teammates enthusiastically followed his direction. Gottlieb, when asked by an audience member how to motivate and inspire young athletes, responded, "I find it best to say 'I really enjoy watching you play.'"

Those words seemed to me to be the best reinforcement one can give any young performer—be it athlete, band member, cheerleader, etc. Those words, given with sincerity, are not just complimentary, but tend to inspire. If the athlete should then ask "What can I do to improve?" the door swings wide open for suggestions.

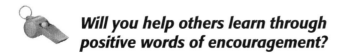

Will you help others learn through positive words of encouragement?

September 28, 2014

After further review …

The sports world is "rocked" with macabre social issues. Sports stars too often take a pass on the opportunity to provide role modeling. Ethics seem dictated by money, and the trappings of fame. So let's turn our attention to many who have daily contact with youth, and work hard to help them grow up to be responsible citizens.

How many young people are provided each day with positive direction by our local and nationwide Boys' and Girls' clubs?

How many lives have been influenced in healthy ways by the people recently honored by our local Community Partnership for Youth for the work they do keeping kids on a positive path?

How many of the 400 youths and adults who attended our local spring Sportsnight were influenced by our guest speaker, Andrew Luck, who pointed out that the average NFL career lasts only 3-and-a-half years, which is why he returns to college in the off-season to stay current in order to be prepared for his post-football years?

How many young people were in the Monterey Peninsula College audience of 300, listening to the challenges presented by former and current NFL head coaches Herm Edwards and Ron Rivera (both locally raised), as they discussed "doing the right thing," and provided real-life examples of how to do it?

How many youths listen to the world-class athletes sponsored by Positive Coaching Alliance, with chapters throughout our nation, encouraging them to follow "ethics in action" in whatever they do?

How many young people have been transformed by our local coaches, teachers, and parents who have been encouraged by Joe Ehrmann, a former NFL player, who has dedicated his life to inspiring role models and instructors to "coach from the inside out?"

How many young people in our community have been provided positive examples of good sportsmanship by our local coaches who have been awarded the Golden Whistle, presented by our local television station and sponsored by a local produce company, for their exemplary service to youth?

These programs, these people, and their commitment are there in thousands of communities from one end of this great land-of-opportunity to the other. Welcome and encouraging news can be found every single day in the world of service to youth in America.

 Will you be part of a program in your community that helps provide positive examples for kids to follow?

9 PERSONAL GROWTH

iStock/Thinkstock

After further review …

"NBA games are too long and the league ought to eliminate halftime," said analyst Jeff Van Gundy during a recent NBA Finals game. His co-analyst Mark Jackson countered, "If they do that, how would you make your halftime adjustments?" Van Gundy, getting in the last word, replied, "If you wait until halftime to make adjustments, you've already lost."

Hmmm? Eliminate halftime? Stay tuned!

First and foremost, the NBA is not of a mindset to do away with that 15-minute break in the action. In actuality, players get about 10 to12 minutes rest time, given the walk to and from their locker rooms and a few warm-up shots prior to the tipoff for the second half.

Dr. Van Gundy, an honorary Doctor of Humane Letters from his alma mater Nazareth College, and a former NBA coach (seven years with the New York Knicks, four with the Houston Rockets), was never heard complaining about the midgame pause when he was coaching. Further, and more to the point, a "breather" is needed to physically recoup, especially with the height and weight of today's athletes. (And from the fans' perspective, time is needed for a trip to the bathroom, replenishing the bowl of nachos and grabbing a beer or two!)

Let's return to the subject of adjustment: coaches are making adjustments, from the opening tipoff to halftime. "Halftime is a management course built right into the game," said former NFL head coach and current ESPN analyst Herm Edwards. Whatever preceded the break, a team is given the opportunity to retreat to a battle-free haven and reassemble its resources. If a team has been successful, they are given a chance to build on that advantage. If they have struggled or been caught unprepared, this halftime "crash-course" gives them a chance to review their shortcomings and start over.

That chance to start over is often all an eventual winner needs. Hence, here's a reminder that each of us needs to take a break in our daily routines that can serve the very same purpose as halftime in athletic contests.

Will you plan a "halftime" in your daily activities to assess your progress?

June 29, 2014

After further review …

Martin Kaymer, the 29-year-old golfer from Dusseldorf, won the U.S. Open played at Pinehurst 2. Kaymer set the 36-hole record at 130 on his way to shooting a 271 for an eight-shot victory. He is the first continental European golfer to win the U.S. Open as his first major title, on only his second attempt.

Pinehurst 2 was a worthy test and made victims of most of the professionals who played. While some might have complained about the restored course with its wire grass and native (sandhill) areas, it was Kaymer who executed great course management.

"We should celebrate what Martin Kaymer did this week," said Mark Davis, USGA Executive Director, who walked the final 18 with the champion.

One of the "victims" of this course was Erik Compton, who finished in a second-place tie at one-under-par with Rickie Fowler. Compton, currently ranked 43rd among professional golfers, has a well-chronicled story as a two-time heart transplant recipient. Yes, you read correctly! Compton, 34, from Miami, had his first heart transplant at age 12 in 1992 due to cardiomyopathy and yet another in 2008. If you're keeping score at home, this is his third heart!

Compton, who won $789,330 for his second-place tie at the Open didn't take his winnings and go on a cruise. No, he showed up at Hartford Hospital in Connecticut to visit other transplant patients, offering words of encouragement. As startling as it may seem, there were 861 double heart transplants performed between 2002 and 2011. Although photographers followed him to the hospital for picture-ops, Compton avoided them with practiced skill.

He said he preferred private time with patients as he did visiting Shawn Fullard who was about to undergo her second heart transplant. He told her that his weight had dropped to 129 pounds following his own second procedure. He assured her that the weight will come back and said: "Stay strong." And oh yes, he left her with his autographed golf glove!

Compton's father once told Erik after the second heart transplant, "You can either consider yourself a 'victim' or 'lucky.'"

 Will you face your challenges without considering yourself a victim?

After further review …

Has anyone ever let you down? Your kids? Your spouse/partner? Your employee? Has the reverse ever occurred? Can you honestly say that you always lived up to the expectations of others?

Current issues in today's sports world have captured the attention of our nation's media. The swirl of instant headlines and commentary has created a rush to judgment. But while each of us is entitled to an opinion, only those granted the responsibility have the right to make those decisions.

Let's take the disciplining of our children as an example. Discipline: "The practice of training people to obey rules or a code of behavior, using punishment to correct disobedience." Who of us has the right to tell other parents how and by what means they must—or must not—teach or discipline their children? Rules and codes are observed differently among families, societies or cultures. That being said …

Corporal punishment that veers into violence should never be acceptable or justifiable, but the matter of degree can be difficult to assess. I was raised by parents and nuns who subscribed to the notion that sparing the rod might spoil the child. The nuns ruler-swatted me on the hands when I misbehaved—unfulfilled expectations? Now, recall your upbringing and tell me you don't, in some way, model your parents' and/or teachers' methodologies? Good, bad, right, or wrong!

The world is full of psychology experts. They never seem to fail to weigh in on the controversial stories of the moment. Many of those same folks watch programs that feature violence; they love race car crashes and graphic slow-mo footage of athletes colliding at full speed—even better with the replays. It is nonsensical for such pseudo experts to whine about "justice" in situations in which they play no part. Better that we concentrate on solutions to prevent domestic violence and child abuse in the future—it's our best option.

Professional sports leagues require rookies to attend three- or four-day symposiums emphasizing social and professional responsibilities. Topics include decision making, mental and physical health, substance abuse, respect for others and for the game, and how to maintain positive relationships. "Holding one's self to a higher standard" is expected of every professional athlete. A noble phrase, but easily forgotten when put to the test. Behavioral change can be done, but it's not a simple one.

Many professional athletes may need to make adjustments in their learned behaviors to comply with the responsibilities set before them. Some may feel too proud to do so or to ask for help. It is important we encourage others to ask for help when they need it. It's one of life's most valuable tools.

 Will you make needed personal adjustments to comply with standards set before you?

September 6, 2015

After further review …

Most of us have not had the distinction of dealing with "the cut man," sometimes called "the Turk." He is often compared to "the Grim Reaper," which folklore describes as either of two characters: the personification of death, generally seen as a tall, often skeletal, specter wearing a black-hooded robe and wielding a sinister scythe when visiting a commoner; or a simple guide who takes you beyond where you are now. Let's focus on that second entity, the guide.

During preseason practices, NFL teams carry nearly 100 players, trying them out to see which ones best fit their plans for that season. As the preseason develops, some players are found to be expendable and released from their contracts. Come the first week of September, some 80 players need to be trimmed to meet the 53-player limit required by league rules. Enter "the cut man," usually an assistant coach or one who assists the general manager. When he knocks on your door, his message is simple: "Coach wants to see you—and bring your playbook." Ouch!

Releasing those final 27, surely-qualified NFL players is the toughest job for an NFL head coach (more on that later). But let's turn our attention to those 27. Tough to hear? You bet! Yet, some 800 players get that knock on the door each September. Those players have dedicated their lives to playing in the NFL. They've planned, worked out, practiced, attended training camps, given their all, and now—football is done, and they are … cut!

How does a head coach handle this exercise? Former head coach and current ESPN analyst Herm Edwards said that "without a doubt it was my most difficult part of the job." Having been a 10-year player and head coach for eight years, he knows that pain. Herm said he always met personally and privately with every player he had to cut. He employed the philosophy, "The possibilities always lie ahead of you—not behind you!"

With every player and in every situation, Herm said he took his time and understanding to help that player plan for his future, sometimes referring him to others who can "guide" him toward a meaningful future.

Will you look ahead for possibilities that will guide you in another direction when faced with the "Grim Reaper"?

After further review …

I am happy that America continues to be, for many, a land of dreams," said Pope Francis, in his remarks this week to Congress. "Dreams which lead to action, to participation, to commitment. Dreams which awaken what is deepest and truest in the life of people."

Sports also figure deeply and truly in the life of the American people: please welcome Josh Robinson, an exemplary citizen on the football field and in this "land of dreams."

Robinson, No. 34, is a running back for the Indianapolis Colts who was drafted in the sixth round of the 2015 NFL draft—pick No. 206, to be exact. Colts head coach Chuck Pagano said, "He's hard to find, being 5-7 and change, but he's tough and competitive." Robinson puts it this way: "I had no parents and no home, but just a big 'ol heart."

Let's back up a bit. He didn't really know his parents, since he had an absent father and a mother who was incarcerated for various offenses. Up stepped his grandmother, who became his stabilizing force and raised him until her untimely death, when he was just 11.

What followed was a series of stays with various family members and friends. Robinson estimates he stayed in 20 different households. One "household" in particular stands out. Robinson lived for six months in the back seat of a hand-me-down Nissan, given to him by his uncle while he was in high school in Franklinton, Louisiana. That's where he was a two-sport athlete in football and track, and led his team to the 4A state championship.

True to that big heart, he never told anyone he was homeless. His football coach, Shane Smith, later said, "Had he told me … believe me, he'd have been staying with me."

Robinson's spirit was never affected by these highly unusual "lack-of-home" circumstances and his enthusiasm is contagious. When Coach Smith explained to him the importance of a playoff game in his junior year, Robinson rushed for 200 yards … in the first half!

He entered Mississippi State University on a Pell Grant, which gave him $2,800 for the entire semester's expenses. However, MSU running back coach Greg Knox held it for him and would dole it out as needed. The coach reasoned that many 18-year-olds with pocket money for the first time rush out, get tattoos and buy rims for their cars.

Not Robinson. At the end of the year he had about $500 left over, so he went home and bought Christmas presents for others. Robinson never let his circumstances detour him. His story is just beginning.

Will you allow your dreams to lead you to action, participation and commitment?

October 25, 2015

After further review …

"I believe the game (Major League Baseball) is globalizing. It's getting influenced by cultures from different parts of the world, and we need to open our minds. We need to accept differences. Differences are good," said Toronto Blue Jays right fielder Jose Bautista.

Bautista, 35, born in Santo Domingo in the Dominican Republic, has played for six different teams, starting out as a utility player. He was traded from the Pittsburgh Pirates to the Blue Jays in 2008, and for the next several seasons became one of the most dominant hitters in baseball. He played in the MLB All-Star game six times and won the Hank Aaron award twice. But his comparison with Aaron stops at that gate.

Being from educated parents—his mother is an accountant and financial planner and his father holds a master's degree in agricultural engineering—Bautista attended a private high school in Santo Domingo and believes so passionately in education that he initiated a program to give athletes the opportunity to attend American universities in the Dominican Republic and Canada. His interest in education, although fostered by his parents, was put to good use when he turned down offers from the Yankees and the Diamondbacks to attend Chipola College in Marianna, Florida, for two years before being drafted by the Pirates 2000.

Bautista's comparison to Aaron fizzled with Bautista's "bat flip" in Game 5 of the ALDS against the Texas Rangers—a sort of "Take that!"—something you would never see from Aaron. No. 44, who ranks second in MLB home runs with 755, never flipped a bat, not even when he broke Babe Ruth's record at 715! Hank simply laid his bat down as he trotted to first base. You see, Hank knew he'd have to come to the plate again and knew better than to antagonize that pitcher.

Bautista has always played with a chip-on-his-shoulder attitude. Perhaps it's because it took him several years to achieve major league status. Aaron surely could have—but didn't—had the same chip-on-the-shoulder approach to life. Born into a poor family at a time when "differences weren't accepted," Aaron entered MLB just two years after Jackie Robinson established those differences. Aaron's MLB legacy is huge by virtue of the numbers he put up, yet it is grounded in humility. As an example, when "Hammerin' Hank" got his 3,000th hit, he said, "It took me 19 years to get that many hits and then, I did it in one afternoon on the golf course." That attitude would serve Bautista well.

 Will you assume Aaron's attitude of gratefulness and humility in your approach to life?

10 SUCCESS

After further review …

The Sports Illustrated Nov. 23 issue featured a story on Caltech athletics, taking specific aim at their current basketball prowess. This was an uncommon SI article, to say the least, and it spoke to me personally. In "Revenge of the Nerds," staff writer Chris Ballard went on to observe, "After decades of ignominious defeats, Caltech finally has a formula for turning the tables on its conference foes." The Beavers, as they are known, play in Division III SCIAC (Southern California Intercollegiate Conference Athletic Conference). "Humiliating" might have been the more familiar word to use, but "ignominious" is more "Caltech-ese." Of course.

Caltech, known formerly as California Institute of Technology, is located in Pasadena, just two miles from where I grew up in San Gabriel. Obviously with that title the college tends to be primarily devoted to the instruction of technical arts and sciences, not athletics. The school, whose motto is "The truth shall make you free," is known more for its Nobel Prize winners (20) than for its Heisman Trophy winners (zero). The Beavers nickname pays homage to nature's engineers—and they are the best!

When I attended Occidental College, also an SCIAC member, I became well acquainted with the athletic programs at Caltech, playing against them in three sports: football (which they canceled after the 1993 season), basketball and baseball. Today, the school offers 19 sports for its students. "OXY" seldom lost to Caltech during my tenure. The Beavers were not much competition for our OXY Tigers in football as we had a bowl-ready team. Caltech was coached by legendary football coach Burt LaBrucherie (erstwhile head football coach at UCLA, his alma mater, and whose Bruins played in the 1947 Rose Bowl Game), yet OXY never lost to them. Ironically, when LaBrucherie became the Beaver's coach in 1949, the Rose Bowl was their home field. The change was dramatic for LaBrucherie since football was highly regarded at UCLA, but not so much at Caltech. LaBrucherie loved coaching as Caltech, but he once observed about his players, "often they would line up with the wrong team." Their focus was clearly elsewhere!

If memory serves me accurately, OXY never lost to Caltech during my four-year basketball career, although their effort (think beavers!) was without question! My admiration for the dedication shown by Caltech student-athletes—then as well as today—is of the utmost. My congratulations to the 11 men on this year's basketball team, who, with GPAs at 3.85 and above (and no athletic scholarships), continue "trying to solve the unsolvable problem."

 Will you support superior students who also honor athletic competition for its value in their education, and later contributions to society?

After further review …

Prior to Game 4 of the NBA Finals, a reporter asked Golden State Warriors head coach Steve Kerr if he was going to make any changes for the next game with the Cleveland Cavaliers. Kerr said there would be no change. At that point the Cavaliers led 2-1 in the best-of-seven series and had home-court advantage at Quicken Loan Arena.

When the teams took the court, it was obvious Kerr had made a major change by starting Draymond Green (6-foot-7) at center in place of 7-foot-0 Andrew Bogut. Kerr also included Andre Iguodala (6-6) in what he termed his "small lineup." It worked, with the Warriors winning 103-82, their largest margin of victory yet over the Cavs. In his post-game interview, Kerr admitted "I lied. I did …," stating his rationale that "If I did tell you the truth, it's equivalent to knocking on the Cavs' head coach's (David Blatt) door and saying, 'Hey, this is what we're going to do.'

"The small lineup made sense since we were getting off to slow starts in the prior games," Kerr explained, "so we did it for pace and floor spacing to get our tempo going."

The strategy worked the way Coach Kerr had planned. However, to sit a couple of your starters can create tension on a team. But not the way face-to-face coach Kerr goes about it. The key is developing a trustworthy and straightforward relationship with each player by fostering an attitude of selfless credit for a team victory. (Incidentally, the Warriors won the final three games to take the series 4-2.)

But what about the lying part? Is it OK for a coach to willingly deceive the press? In Kerr's case, he went directly to the questioning reporter after the game and apologized. The reporter, in turn, accepted the apology. The key in any relationship is that clear and simple term: straightforwardness. ('Course, it does help if you win!) Most reporters are as competitive as the athletes, and want the "edge" in getting their story out first. This can lead to over-inquisitive questioning of a coach sitting on the firing line.

Will you grant Coach Kerr this "fib," since he used it to prevent an opponent from gaining an advantage?

After further review …

"In God we trust?" In some quarters of society those four words have become more of a question than a statement of belief. In 1861 Samuel P. Chase, secretary of the U.S. Treasury, instructed James Pollock, director of the Philadelphia Mint, to inscribe those words on coins with this note:" Dear Sirs: No nation can be strong except in the strength of God or safe except in His defense. The trust of our people in God should be so declared on our national coins." While it serves as our nation's motto and is respected by the vast majority, the practice of expressing it has come under fire.

An assistant football coach at Bremerton High School in Washington state is currently on paid administrative leave for praying with his team at midfield after their games. District officials took that action after warning him to stop, saying that students who were not present or didn't wish to participate in that ritual would necessarily "suffer a degree of coercion to participate in a religious activity when their coaches lead or endorse it." The Seattle chapter of the Satanic Temple had filed a protest seeking to prohibit that postgame activity.

What constitutes prayer in those postgame ceremonies is unknown, and beside the point, for the view here is it not "religious" if its specific intent is to enhance the group identity of players sharing a common goal. It is doubtful that the "prayer" probes the depth or sincerity of any individual's relationship with a higher power. How can one protest an exercise in togetherness that is designed to strengthen a team?

Being in locker rooms and on fields before and after games, I have witnessed hundreds of these kinds of activities. It has been my observation that what is being said and professed is a summoning of one's inner strength and determination in order to help them perform better, or a gesture of gratitude for having the opportunity to perform their duties.

The opinion here is that a safe and successful performance of one's job is not, or shouldn't be, dependent on a prayer for winning. Any prayer to God to win, demands, by definition, the devaluation an opponent. God doesn't work that way. It would put God in an impossible position whenever Notre Dame plays Boston College, both Catholic-based universities! Former President Ronald Reagan put it this way: "The Constitution was never meant to prevent people from praying; its declared purpose was to protect their freedom to pray."

 Will you log in to express your opinion about Bremerton High School's administrative decision?

October 18, 2015

After further review …

It's an American tradition that's part of our folklore: after mom or grandma planned, prepared, cooked and served the big family dinner on Sunday afternoon, while the dishes were being cleared, she would say, "Keep your fork!" To all those crowded around the table that meant, "Yum, somethin's good's a-comin'!" Some might visualize it as pie a la mode, or chocolate cake, but whatever lay ahead, it was gonna be good! Perhaps that's what Chicago Cubs fans are thinking today, having kept their forks close at hand for decades.

As we approach midseason in the high school, college and/or professional football worlds, some fans have begun to lose confidence in their team. They've already put away their forks! A few fans have even said they're not sure it's football their team is playing, that it's more like a bunch of people wandering around the pasture looking for their lost keys.

Is your team's season over and it's still October? Have you abandoned them because they've already lost more games than they have won and, thus, been pretty much eliminated from the playoffs? Is that why fans attend games—for the playoffs? Are today's fans too finicky? If members of your family were playing or coaching, would you abandon them if they were losing?

Herm Edwards, former head coach of the New York Jets (and subsequent head coach of the Kansas City Chiefs, now an ESPN analyst) is clear on this topic. In his rookie season as a head coach in 2001 the Jets finished 9-7, a good start. However, in October 2002 his team was 1-3 and the coach was facing a room of frustrated New York reporters. One of the reporter's questions strongly implied that the 2002 season was lost; was Coach Edwards thinking of abandoning this season to prepare for the next? Edwards' response was classic Herm!

"You play to win the game!"

"Hello?"

"You play to win the game! That's the great thing about sports, you play to win. I don't care if you don't have any wins, you play to win! If you're telling me, it doesn't matter, get out, 'cause it does matter!" Edwards' response was emphatic. It's a central belief of his, throughout his playing and coaching career, and in his personal career as well. "There's no quit in my dictionary," he has often said. "The possibilities always lie ahead of you, not behind you!"

 Will you follow the Edwards Code and "keep your fork?"

After further review …

The story of the 2015 Brigham Young University football team is still a work in progress. The twist of fate responsible for the Cougars' auspicious beginning this season is one typically told toward the end of a bruising season. Let me explain.

BYU's starting quarterback, Taysom Hill, is a senior and highly respected in college football ranks. In the season opener against the Nebraska Cornhuskers, Hill broke his foot (it's called a Lisfrance sprain) and is lost for the season. Enter Tanner Mangum, a redshirt freshman.

Mangum, was a widely recruited quarterback from Eagle, Idaho. Seven major college football schools were offering scholarships, but Mangum chose BYU. Then he spent two years performing his Mormon mission, the last three months in the Antofagasta region of Chile. He hadn't suited up for four years, and now, with starting quarterback Hill on the bench with a broken foot, Mangum walks onto the hallowed football gridiron in Lincoln to face the Nebraska Cornhuskers.

With 48 seconds left on the game clock, the Cougars were on their own 24 yard line, behind in the score 28-27; Mangum drove his team to the Cornhuskers' 42, with a single second remaining. From there he launched a "Hail Mary" (a traditional Catholic prayer, but a suitable tactic for Mormons or Methodists in desperate situations) toward the end zone, where 6-6" Mitch Mathews outjumped two Cornhusker defenders for the winning catch. BYU wins 34-28 and Nebraska loses its first home game opener in 30 years! This is playground fantasy stuff!

Mangum is not done yet. The next week, now the starting quarterback, he is facing the Boise State Broncos in LaVell Edwards Stadium—home field of the Cougars. Hmm, three short months ago Mangum was in Chile working for the Church of Latter-day Saints. Mangum struggled against the Broncos most of the game; as the fourth quarter began, Boise State led by 10. But Mangum and the Cougars never gave up! With only 45 seconds left, Mangum threw a 35-yard touchdown pass to Mitchell Juergens. Cougars win 35-24. Guess it doesn't matter whether your name is Mitch or Mitchell as long as a guy named Tanner is throwing the football. Back-to-back Hail Marys!

The essence of this is Mangum giving credit to faith in himself. He describes his early season success as "keeping your cool and doing the best you can so you can help others around you."

 Will you maintain faith in yourself so you can help others?

After further review …

Growing up in Pebble Beach has to be a fortunate circumstance. Pebble Beach has the aura of paradise throughout much of the world, and especially the world of golf. With a family home situated on the first fairway of one of the most famous golf courses in the world, one could be forgiven for feeling somehow special, or endowed with "certain unalienable rights." That's one highly prized backyard!

W. Lawson Little III was that fortunate resident. But he never translated it that way, never thought in those terms. He never considered himself special or entitled in any way. Yet, he was special, though by a completely different measure. Lawson III, who died recently of the rare blood disorder septicemia, had a special gift for making everyone he met feel uniquely deserving. He was a lifelong talented athlete, as competitive as they come, but his most dominant characteristic was helping others.

His father, W. Lawson Little Jr., was considered by many as the "most dominant amateur golfer in the history of the game." He won the U.S. Amateur and the British Amateur tournaments back-to-back in 1935 and 1936, a feat known in the golfing world as the Little Slam—it was, indeed, the "Little" slam! He won 32 consecutive matches during that time. In 1935, Jr. was awarded the prestigious Sullivan Award as amateur of the year. Turning professional in 1936, he won the U.S. Open in 1940, and, was inducted (posthumously) into the World Golf Hall of Fame in 1980.

With that history of golfing celebrity illuminating his background, "Laws" (as we called him) never "piggybacked" on his father's fame. Laws' own claim to fame was what he did for his family and for virtually everyone he encountered. Laws picked up golf balls and worked in the pro shop at Quail Lodge Resort and Golf Club (Carmel Valley) as he earned his way through life. He ventured into real estate and developed Quail Meadows, considered one of the finest properties in the valley. He later became the President of Quail Lodge Resort and Golf Club.

Laws raised a lot of money for local charities via signature events that he brought to Quail Lodge: The Quail, a Motorsports Gathering; The Quail Rally; and The Eagle Cup. He was a contributing board member of the Jim Tunney Youth Foundation, and was instrumental in fundraising for local community youth organizations. He served on many community boards.

In 2009, Laws was awarded "Ambassador of the Year" by the California Golf Writers Hall of Fame, an honor he neither sought nor talked about. He will be remembered as a friend and a goodwill ambassador with a loving spirit and a lifetime of giving. Laws never remembered what he gave, but never forgot what he was given.

 Will you pattern your life by helping others as Laws did?

After further review …

For 31 years on the NFL field, my responsibility was to ensure that justice was done with integrity. It was never important to me what T*E*A*M won, but that the game was played fairly and within the rules. The same principle held true on the campus in my role as teacher or principal. Justice had to be meted out fairly.

Being in the school building for more than 30 years, it was important for me to support, guide and encourage students to do the right thing. Yet, people find ways to manipulate the facts to "cover their tracks." These behaviors are mostly learned from others, not inherited. About two years ago I read about when Brian Banks finally was exonerated and walked out of the courtroom a free man with his head held high. Although elated, the false crime bothered me.

Here's the story: In 2002, Banks was arrested and charged with rape. Allegedly, Banks, a promising high school football star, dragged a female classmate into the school stairwell and had forcible sex with her. Faced with the possibility of a 40-years-to-life sentence, Banks' lawyer persuaded him to accept a plea deal that put him behind bars for 62 months, to be followed by five years of probation. The remainder of his life would be lived as a registered sex offender and branded with an electronic monitor. Banks' dream of playing college (the University of Southern California had offered him a scholarship), and hopefully in the NFL, was shattered.

The victim's family sued the school district and won a $1.5 million dollar settlement. However, once released from prison Banks was added as a friend on Facebook by the victim who said she made up the rape charge and admitted that what happened was consensual. (Note: As the result of Banks' exoneration, the school district has recouped the money). But where is the justice for Banks?

The proliferation of child molestation, domestic violence and sexual assault today is beyond anything expected in a civilized society. The damage done to the victims is tragic and lifelong. Given the nature of sexual assaults, we tend to side with the victims. Justice, however, must serve both sides.

Banks has "moved on." His dream of being in the NFL, in a sense, has been fulfilled, but not on the field. Banks is now employed in the football operations department of the NFL and helping in the officiating department on game days.

"I am honored to say I have taken an amazing position with the NFL. God is good," Banks said.

 How will you handle an injustice that may come your way?

After further review …

What are the odds that a black kid born to a 25-year-old mother, who already had five children, who had been an alcoholic since she was 14 and during this pregnancy spent most of her welfare check on crack cocaine, would even live? Or if he did live, would spend much of his life engulfed with an addiction? Two of his brothers never lived beyond 29 years of age. His mother, yes, that mother, died in a house fire—set by another 16-year-old son!

Reading the wonderful, heart-warming story written by S.L. Price in Sports Illustrated (Nov. 10), you have the feeling that anyone can find a way to beat the odds. Surf the channels this college basketball season to find West Point, the U.S. Military Academy and look for number "0," which is the number worn by Max Lenox. He won't be in the starting lineup, although he is Army's co-captain. Lenox is the black kid mentioned above. And "zero" is the appropriate number, which, at birth, appeared to be his chances for survival.

The West Point campus is filled with all-staters and future Rhodes scholars, but this 6-foot, 200-pound Lenox, who averaged six minutes (not points) a game last season, is co-captain because he is "very special," according to his teammates. When you watch Max play, you may notice that he has heavy knee pads (braces-like) on both knees from a torn meniscus that happened in high school.

A kid like Max needs help and that is exactly what he got from his parents: Dave Lenox and Nathan Merrells, two gay partners, who adopted Max early-on. Both Dave and Nathan are successful men in their own right, but their hearts went out to Max. They nurtured him throughout his learning disabilities and his failure of two classes at West Point, which forced him to be a "turnback" cadet and repeat his plebe year. Then being raised by gay parents—well, it has not been an easy journey.

When told of this background one coach said, "I don't care. But if he's a good kid, I'll take him." Max is just that and lives by T.E. Lawrence's words: "All men dream: but not equally. The dreamers of the day are dangerous men, for they act their dreams with open eyes, to make it possible." Max recites that daily.

Will you dream with your eyes open to beat the odds you may be facing?

After further review …

Now that several billion people have had their fill of soccer's 2014 FIFA World Cup—for which an appropriate refrain might be "Don't cry for me, Argentina"—perhaps their attention can now turn to those other worldly topics: free agency and tenure. Can we find a parallel between these two employment issues in the worlds of sport and education?

"Free agency" generally describes a professional player who is free of contract terms with any other team, and therefore eligible to sign with a new team of his choosing. This particular issue is a highly complicated one, full of conditions and restrictions, and too unwieldy for a full explanation here. But when a team drafts a player and signs him to a long-term contract, shouldn't that player be required to remain with that team until his playing days are over? At one point in sports history that was the case. Why did the system change to favor the players, rather than the owners who provide them the opportunity to play professionally?

Many believe the answer to that question to be "because that's called slavery." St. Louis Cardinals outfielder Curt Flood took his refusal of a trade to Philadelphia all the way to the U.S. Supreme Court in 1969, and though he lost, his case paved the way for the abolishment of Major League Baseball's reserve clause. Free agency followed, allowing players much greater freedom to take their talents wherever they want. The exorbitant market values enjoyed by many current players never existed before there was open competition for their services.

In the business world, employees are free to change jobs at will. In the education world the safeguard for teachers is the law of tenure, which guarantees employment after a probationary period has been satisfied. Many today claim that tenure only protects the underperforming teacher. The qualified teacher, they say, doesn't need such protection.

But who can sit in absolute judgment of a teacher's worth? Learning in today's world is not confined to the classroom, or to arbitrary standards of achievement. Learning takes place 24/7/365. A good teacher is there to guide students through the maze of modern life.

In the sports world, players making the most of their personal improvement give their teams the best chance to win. The same is true in education, with the "winners" being the students.

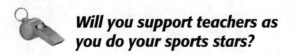

***Will you support teachers as
you do your sports stars?***

September 7, 2014

After further review …

"Now batting (pause) shortstop (pause) numbah two (pause) Derek Jee-tah (pause) numbah two." Thus spoke the legendary New York Yankees public address announcer Bob Sheppard, every time "The Captain" approached the plate. This month of September will comprise the final at bats for the 20-year Yankee veteran. Sheppard died in 2010, just 100 days short of his 100th birthday, yet Jeter continued to use that recorded introduction every time he stepped into the batter's box at Yankee Stadium with Sheppard's dignified monotone and just a touch of "New Yawk."

Because of Jeter's tireless clutch performances on the field, both are legends in my mind. The genesis of my admiration occurred around the age of 9 or 10 when I became a Yankees fan. Each night as I went to bed listening to the voice of Mel Allen on the radio (television was still a rookie), he announced the names of Joe DiMaggio, Lou Gehrig, Red Ruffing and many other exalted Yankees. My dream as a young ball player was to pitch for the Yankees—an ambition never reached.

However, I did stand on the mound at the original Yankee stadium. No, I wasn't the starting pitcher, or even a reliever, and no, the Yankees weren't playing. 1960 was my first year as an NFL official. I was assigned as the field judge for a game between the Pittsburgh Steelers and the New York Giants. Our officiating crew of five took the "D" train from mid-Manhattan to the Bronx and walked a couple of blocks to the stadium locker room entrance.

Arriving in the officials' locker room, I set my officiating bag down and walked down the tunnel, into the first base dugout (the one the Yankees used), up four steps and straight to the pitcher's mound. The mound had been removed as it was in the end zone of the football field, but I took a stretch windup and threw the imaginary pitch right down the pipe!

Sheppard was also the announcer for the New York Giants. I can still hear (and feel) his smooth and distinctively-timed elocution describing an offensive foray: "Gifford (pause) right tackle (pause) for six." Sheppard and Jeter are forever linked in my mind as true practitioners of Yankee class, whether or not they get plaques in Monument Park.

Will you aspire to the understated excellence of Sheppard and Jeter?

11 TEAMWORK

After further review …

Are we getting an overabundance of curtain calls in sporting events? Perhaps you love stage plays as much or more than I do. Whether it be on Broadway or on the Morgan Stock stage at Monterey Peninsula College, the joy and excitement of actors performing live is hard to beat. When the principal actor appears on stage for the first time, there is polite applause. While the actor may feel that honor, he or she proceeds directly into the assigned role. At the conclusion of the play, actors are called on-stage for a curtain call. Recognition of a stellar performance is often greeted with a standing ovation.

This leads to today's professional athletes: are they overdoing curtain calls? Being around professional athletes most of my adult life, I have great admiration for their skills and athleticism. However, today's athletes seem to want recognition before, during and after every part of their performance. Their introductions with "bells and whistles" and "rockets-red-glare" are over the top.

People wonder, what's with the fist-pounding-of-the-chest after a "slam dunk" by a player whose normal reach is beyond the rim? Or the catching of a forward pass followed by the first-down signal … isn't that the officials' job? Or (more) pounding of the chest or flexing of muscles—a la Charles Atlas—after sacking the quarterback? Many ask, isn't that what they are there for? Then, of course, those big brother examples of "showmanship" trickle down to high schools and Little Leaguers.

It has often been said, "Sports builds character," to which came the reply, "Well, it may not build character, but it certainly can reveal it." The contention here is that sports are a great way to learn teamwork, to learn to give your best effort every time, to not quit when you think you can't do more, to learn to respect others for their efforts, and to be grateful for the opportunity. If and when the curtain call comes, one needs to accept that recognition with humility!

As we approach this week of Thanksgiving, can we regularly maintain the gratefulness of which that day reminds us?

 Will you continue to be grateful for the opportunities you've been given?

November 3, 2013

After further review …

A recurring theme (and a very strong suggestion) in my presentations to corporate, business and education groups is this: "Catch people doing something right!"

When one makes a mistake or is not working to one's potential, others of us tend to be caustic in our immediate judgment of their performance or behavior. Does that promote growth? The suggestion here is to reward others when they are doing the right thing. The idea is to eliminate errors and build confidence. Incidentally, it's of no value to say "build-up." Where people are concerned, that's the only direction there is. Lifted up, raised to a new state of being.

The impetus of this message came as I witnessed players and coaches (at all levels) berating teammates in an attempt to improve performance, which all too often made recipients defensive. A better approach is the positive application of criticism. The word "criticism" is often defined as "finding fault" with such synonyms as "rap," "swipe," "flak," "knock," all pejorative.

In building his team one coach has said "It's about holding people accountable, and with that comes a little pushing, and prodding—and a lot of patting them on the back." Sounds like catching people doing something right fits well with that coach's philosophy. Outside of athletics and the constant need for motivation, these ideas apply to all facets of life, including the raising of your children. Discussing this with one of our daughters recently, she told me her daughter (age 12) needed some "pushing and prodding" to get her homework completed and turned in on time. Hmm, you too?

My experience as an inner-city high school principal prompted me to encourage teachers to take the coach's approach in their classrooms. The thought then—as now—was that their 30-plus students were not all the same and need different kinds of motivation to improve performance. I suggested that some students may be quarterbacks, some running backs, some linemen, i.e., playing different roles. Thus the pushing and prodding and pats on the back will vary from student to student. It has often been a mantra of mine that "there is nothing so unequal as the equal treatment of unequals."

A teacher/parent/coach needs to be stern, but fair in the disciplining of others. A quiet, yet firm voice praising the right thing will build respect. Screaming, yelling, and berating not so much.

 Will you look for ways to catch others doing something right?

After further review …

Recently, the teenage son of one of our On the TUNNEYSIDE of Sports subscribers emailed me, saying that he had just been elected captain of his T*E*A*M. He asked what advice I could give him in order to be successful. Good question.

Firstly, the C in the word captain is important. The C represents the word charge, as in, "You are in charge!" That means it starts with you. The old saw says the "buck stops here" and it's you it has in mind. Let's look at a few C's that may help define the success for you and your T*E*A*M.

Credibility is synonymous with believability, which is marked by trust. Trust starts with you trusting yourself and your good judgment. Good judgment is doing the right thing every time. Your integrity must be transparent. No one typifies that word more my lifelong friend and NFL colleague Art McNally. The NFL recently honored McNally by naming its officiating department's Command Center after him. I wrote many years ago that I would play poker over the phone with Art McNally. That's a goal we all must achieve!

Another C word is courage. It takes guts to step up and be a leader, and that's what you are as captain—a leader. At times you may have fear in-your-belly, and that's normal. But you must fight through that fear. In the movie "Nobody's Fool," Sully, played by the late actor Paul Newman, asked his fearful grandson, "Can you be strong for just one minute?" In the face of a fearful situation, be strong for one minute—at a time.

C also invokes companionship. You can't be a leader by yourself. Steve Young, the San Francisco 49ers' Hall of Fame quarterback, once told me "If you play alone, you'll be alone!" For any quarterback to be successful he must have good running backs, strong offensive linemen, as well as a corps of competent receivers. The same is true for any baseball pitcher, who must have great fielders and hitters to complement his pitching prowess. You need them as much as they need you to be their leader.

And finally, the word quit (different letter, same sound); something you should never do. The suggestion here is not to give up on others too soon, especially when they have a negative performance. That's the very minute when you, the leader, need to step up and boost their courage and strength. Please remember that you lead by example, not just by your words.

 Will you step up with your strengths when granted the captain's role?

April 21, 2014

After further review …

Major league baseball season has begun and once again, a few delusional fans have run onto the field flinging themselves into games. Problem is, they don't have MLB contracts, and have no earthly business on those diamonds. This reminds me of a discussion my grandson and I had when he was playing on his high school baseball team. He was concerned, as a teenager, about the behavior of parents at his games. It bothered him that adults—from both sides—would loudly berate his teammates when mistakes were made.

When I played, coached, and officiated, the thinking was that school games should be different from the pros. What we have witnessed in the last 20-plus years is that both the players and the fans at school games want to emulate those in the pro ranks. Can we trace the blame for this attitude to the "wanna-be" urge?

Sociologists say society today is less respectful of authority. Has the emergence of individual rights (and an accompanying sense of self-entitlement) overridden respect for the rules that are there to benefit all? Booing in sporting events has always been the norm, but have we overcome the restraints that keep it in check? How do we ensure the "rights" of the majority to practice decency and fairness?

Sports have always been the place to learn self-discipline, self-sacrifice, mental toughness and teamwork. There is a wealth of evidence suggesting lessons learned on the playing field translate directly to the home, the family and the workplace. Being on a team—whether it be sports, band, cheerleading, etc.—helps people treat others with respect. Yet it does require the courageous attention of parents, teachers, players, coaches and officials to enforce civility.

It also takes courage, when abuse is hurled your way, not to respond in kind. My experience in athletics brought that fully to my attention. Responding in kind only brought me down to that level. It was always my intention to treat others with respect, no matter how they treated me. By ignoring abuse and walking away, I had greater control over myself and the situation. Respecting others even when they act badly toward you is sportsmanship in its fullest form.

 Will you maintain your dignity in spite of how you are being treated?

After further review …

The major league baseball season is now at its peak, and 30 clubs have been reduced to a final pair—the San Francisco Giants and the Kansas City Royals—focused with rapt attention on the World Series. Did those teams that have been eliminated have trouble with the curve? Clint Eastwood directed and played a major role in his movie "Trouble With the Curve" a couple of years back.

The idea behind "Trouble With the Curve" is that a team needs to employ players who can hit a breaking ball, or as it's more commonly known, "the curve." In the film, Gus, a baseball scout played by Eastwood, is adamant with owners, favoring a recruit who has trouble hitting a curveball.

To illustrate, when a player batting from the left side of the plate faces a left-handed pitcher who throws a wicked curve ball, it appears that the ball is coming straight for his head at around 85 mph before breaking away and dropping into the catcher's mitt. It takes tremendous, knee-knocking courage for a batter to stand there believing that the pitch will break away from him. The change-up is another challenging pitch often seriously disrupting a hitter's judgment and timing.

Segue to your life—how do you handle change? Is it as frightening to you as a curveball spinning toward your head? Do you have the courage to deal with change when it comes your way? Are your knees knocking as batters' may be? Change is inevitable. Batters know and believe that a different pitch is always forthcoming, and find ways to adjust to it. Will you?

Here are a couple of ideas: First and foremost, you must believe the only constant in life is change. When you convince yourself of that, then you can begin to prepare for it. A batter anticipates change. Each of us needs to do the same. Further, if you want to improve yourself physically, mentally, emotionally, financially and spiritually, you must grow toward that which you want to be. In order to grow, we must change. Remaining in one's comfort zone denies the opportunity to improve.

 Will you embrace change when it comes your way?

After further review …

"Ya gotta believe" is a recurring chant in today's sports world. It's written on signs that are waved by fans all over the country.

"November is moving month," says Herm Edwards, former NFL coach and current ESPN analyst, carrying the message one level deeper; if NFL teams are destined for the playoffs, they have to start believing in it now.

November is a major month in the sports world. NFL teams are beyond the halfway point in their season. The NHL is in full swing. The NBA is well underway. College football is accelerating towards its bowl season. College basketball has "tipped-off." And let's not forget soccer, which is in full kick domestically and globally. Wow! It's exciting just writing about it.

Every player, every T*E*A*M, and every fan subscribes to the motto above "Ya gotta believe," but not all succeed at it. Why? Perhaps the answer can be found in Edwards' book "It's the Will, Not the Skill" wherein he expresses his principals and philosophies of success. Edwards says that while every NFL squad has 53 skilled players, each must possess the will to work together as a T*E*A*M. That will is vital to their common goal.

Does this philosophy work outside the world of sports? Of course it does! It counts for students and business people and something as simple as building a sand castle! A few years back while running on the beach near my home, I stopped to watch a young boy, 8 or 9 years old building a sand castle. He didn't understand the incoming tide, and was flabbergasted when a wave ran up the sand and wiped out his castle.

Scrambling on his hands and knees he gathered more sand and was rebuilding his castle, only to have another wave demolish it. This process was repeated a few more times. There was undeniable joy in the rebuilding, but more important, this boy believed he could build another!

It was his attitude and belief that was important to the success of this experience. There was no parent, teacher or coach to push him onward—the encouragement he gave himself made all the difference. Note that the word "encouragement" shelters c-o-u-r-a-g-e, which by definition is "an ability to conquer fear or despair." That is the essence of "Ya gotta believe!"

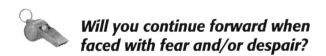

Will you continue forward when faced with fear and/or despair?

12 VALUES

After further review …

Coming up soon, March 4 is Sportsmanship Day. Do we really need to designate a day to remind us all, not just athletes, to be good sports?

How do we measure the value of Sportsmanship Day compared, say, to the recent Presidents Day? Or Valentine's Day? How about later in the year as we honor out parents with Mother's Day or Father's Day. And let's not forget Grandma and Grandpa; they have their day too.

The thinking here is that sportsmanship ought to be observed 24/7. As legendary Notre Dame football coach Knute Rockne often said, "One man practicing good sportsmanship is far better than 50 others preaching it." Got it, coach.

Those words apply to all the above; practice what you would honor on that special day, every day. Sports can help us put into practice what we believe.

One of the intrinsic values of playground sports that many of us played as kids is that we played without referees/umpires or even coaches. During our playground basketball games, we called fouls on ourselves. In our sandlot baseball games, when disputes arose between runners ("I was safe!") and fielders ("Nuh-uh, I tagged ya!") we had to settle them ourselves. And we had to do it quickly since we were usually running out of daylight. Arguing at length was not tolerated.

The value of playing sports cannot be minimized, if just for that reason. English, math and science offer few opportunities to practice sportsmanship. The greatest value of sports is not in proclaiming how talented you are or how many games you won, but the opportunity to practice playing fair. Maybe it's the only classroom that can teach that virtue.

But that virtue needs to be practiced in all our daily activities. It is civility at its best. We ignore the merit of sportsmanship when we cut into a line unfairly or cut someone off in traffic, or belittle others for the sake of our own egos. True sportsmanship, no matter where it originates, is an ethos, an underlying sense of character, which we all need in our daily lives.

 Will you model good sportsmanship and help others understand its value?

August 23, 2015

After further review …

With the fall sports season about to get under way, some coaches and players feel that developing hatred, or at least an aggressive anger, toward opponents is a necessary component for winning. Animosity has no place in sports! Intensity is essential, but let's not get those two states of mind mixed up!

Coaches, in the attempt to get their teams psyched up for a season or a game, frequently resort to fiery incitement and use hate as a tool to build intensity under the guise of T*E*A*M spirit. Wrong! While team spirit is vital for its power to build camaraderie it must be kept in perspective. It's an "I've got your back" mantra that pulls individuals together; it doesn't need to accomplish this by diminishing opponents. The value of sports can be lifelong. The current players on the PGA Tour are providing a positive example of sportsmanship. Recent thumbs-up gestures from Jordan Spieth, and similar examples from Jason Day and Rory McElroy are signs of respect for their opponents. Sure they want to win, but they are mindful that they treat their rivals the way they want to be treated.

Values built on competitiveness guided by honesty and respect are transferable to whatever one does in life. While those mentioned compete as individuals, they treat each other as if they were family. Respecting one's opponent, especially in stressful situations, is a sign of maturity. Maturity, BTW, is not necessarily commensurate with age. The very young can show mature behavior, if given the proper example.

Teamwork, on and off the field, replaces self-importance and ego for the good of others. Steve Young, the Hall of Fame quarterback of the San Francisco 49ers, once said, "If you play alone you'll be alone."

Even in individual sports there needs to be a feeling of T*E*A*M, and indeed, there is often an unseen network of support behind an individual performance. As you strive for your goal, focus your efforts on preparation. The secret is preparation, thorough and complete. The old saw, "The will to prepare is more important than the will to win" can provide the necessary intensity. This prayerful poem taught to me by my father may say it all:

- Dear Lord, in the battle that goes on through life I ask only for a field that is fair
- A chance that is equal to all in the strife, the courage to strive and to dare
- And if I should win, let it be by the code with my faith and my honor held high
- But if I should lose, let me stand by the road and cheer as the winners go by.

 Will you treat your opponents with the same respect that you deserve?

April 19, 2015

After further review …

We can't move on to another topic before we highlight the amazing play of the 55 professional golfers who completed the Masters recently at Augusta. From the opening drives of Gary Player (3), Arnold Palmer (4) and Jack Nicklaus (6)—three past champions who account for 13 Masters titles—to the final round of the 79th champion, Jordan Spieth, it was a special tournament.

There have been many Masters champions who have displayed courage, composure, humility and sportsmanship over these 79 years, but the style and grace of 21-year-old Spieth stands out as a model for all athletes to follow. His thumbs-up gesture at the seventh hole in the final round said it best. Spieth, the leader after the third round with a score of 200 (16 under par), was coupled with Justin Rose, who was 12 under. While one might use the term "partnered with," they were not partners in the sense of playing on the same team, but were direct competitors who teed off and walked the course together.

Spieth not only won the tournament, but he set the following records: lowest score (64) in the opening round, lowest score (130) after the first two rounds and lowest score (200) after the third. He was the only golfer to make 28 birdies in the tournament. Aside from that, he happens to be the second-youngest golfer ever to win the Masters.

But it was in the fourth round that Spieth displayed a sportsmanlike gesture that truly sets him apart. Spieth, laying two, was standing on the edge of the par-4 seventh hole waiting for Rose to hit his third shot, which he was playing from the rough. Rose hit a spectacular shot that landed on the green, and the CBS camera panned to where Spieth was standing and captured him giving Rose the thumbs-up. How many athletes in a highly competitive environment would even think to pay recognition to a competitor's accomplishment, let alone display it on national television? Rose went on to par that hole, but Spieth shot a 5 for a bogey.

"That's what he (Jordan) is," said his father, Shawn. "He appreciates great play as well as other people who play the game right."

Jordan, wearing his green jacket, said in the press conference that followed, "When my competitor is playing, I don't say 'I hope he misses,' not at all. I say to myself, 'I hope he makes it and I will follow by making my shot too.'"

Incidentally, Spieth dropped out of the University of Texas in this, his senior year, to concentrate on golf. By doing so he failed to get his bachelor's degree … but he did earn his Masters!

 Will you treat others with the Spieth code of sportsmanship?

After further review …

With the civil unrest breeding violence around the country, the idea that law enforcement officers should be equipped with body cameras so that potential encounters can be recorded is gaining lots of support. City government officials and state legislators are debating guidelines about the use of such equipment.

Questions accompany this issue. Will cameras be a deterrent? Can they replace trust? Can we draw parallels with other uses of this technology? Stay tuned.

Video replay has found its way into all professional sports and, if mom and pop had the resources, it would be a feature in Little League games as well. Replay will proliferate in sporting events as time marches on. Is it a good thing or not? That's a moot question, since it is common now and viewers are used to it. That's all that counts.

The use of instant replay, as an aid to officiating, began in the National Football League in 1986 (yes, the use of video replay for correcting possible errors is now in its 30th year). There were many opposed to its introduction. Football purists saw it as an intrusion, saying the game is played by people and should be judged that way. Some on-field officials felt similarly. I thought a different approach was necessary, since it was soon apparent that replay was here to stay. The challenge was for game officials to step up their commitment and work ethic to insure that every call was made to perfect standards. By doing so we could possibly reduce the involvement of the replay. And though perfection would seem to be an impossible goal, as head coach emeritus Vince Lombardi of the Green Bay Packers used to tell his players: "Gentlemen, we will relentlessly chase perfection, knowing all the while we can never attain it. But along the way we shall catch excellence." And excellence is what everyone wants to see in a performer, or an official, or a public servant.

Speaking to corporate conventions as well as to players, coaches and game officials, I stress that the No. 1 factor in leadership is trust. While we often trust the camera ("The camera doesn't lie" is an often-quoted maxim), we must develop trust in human beings. In football, for example, quarterbacks must trust their blockers to do their job with excellence. This holds true throughout the sports world, and in life as well.

Will you trust others when they are doing their job to the best of their abilities?

After further review …

February is an exciting month on the Monterey Peninsula. The PGA tour departed from the Hawaiian Islands, blew through the Arizona desert, paused in La Jolla and now arrives in Pebble Beach as the AT&T Pro-Am gets underway. National attention to golf will intensify.

This is always the time of year when beloved golf films like "The Legend of Bagger Vance" and "Tin Cup" come off the shelf. So this story is about a mulligan—a word not in a professional golfer's vocabulary.

A mulligan is defined by some as a "do over," as in a golfer who hits a shot that he/she doesn't like, and drops another ball to do it over. In tournament golf, mulligans are taboo! But among weekend warriors hacking their way through a Saturday morning round, they're plentiful.

A mulligan was allowed recently in the game of tennis. Again, for those who play a friendly game of tennis each morning and a faulty serve occurs, a do-over is often acceptable. Ironically, it is allowed in professional tennis as well, although it almost never happens, except…

The 2015 Australian Open in Melbourne was won by Novak Djokovic (his fifth) over Andy Murray in five sets. But the real story in this event belongs to Tim Smyczek. Who?

Tim Smyczek (he needs to buy a couple of vowels from Vanna White, but saying "Smee-Ckeck" gets his attention) is from Hales Corner, Wisconsin—not a hotbed of tennis.

Smyczek, 27, a certified tennis professional, is ranked 103rd in the world by ATP. At that ranking he must qualify to get into the main draw of this tournament, which he did. He battled through an early round to set up a second-round match with Rafael Nadal, currently ranked third. The match looked like an easy win for Nadal. But, Smyczek took the match to a tie after four sets, 6-2, 3-6, 6-7(2), 6-3.

In the fifth set, Nadal was leading 6-5, serving at 30-love and about to rock his lefty service motion. As he made his toss some yo-yo in the stands loudly shouted something indiscernible. It startled Nadal, whose serve was long. Nadal's tough luck? Not to Smyczek, who approached the chair umpire and offered Nadal a mulligan based on the fan's disruption.

Able to repeat his first serve, Nadal went on the win the point, the game, the set (7-5) and the match. Smyczek said afterward, "It was just the right thing to do."

 Will you consider Smyczek's sportsmanship in whatever you do?

January 11, 2015

After further review …

This piece is being written on Friday before the NFC Divisional playoff game on Sunday between the Dallas Cowboys and the Green Bay Packers in historic Lambeau Field in Green Bay, Wisconsin. This was the first time the Cowboys had played in a playoff game in Green Bay since 1967. The National Weather Service predicted a game-time temperature of 15 degrees.

I was part of the eight-man NFL officiating crew (six on-field with two alternates, one of whom was me) that arrived in Green Bay on Saturday, Dec. 30, 1967, for the NFL Championship game. This was prior to the merger of the two professional football leagues, with the winner meeting the AFL champion in the AFL-NFL World Championship game, which it was called before the name was changed to Super Bowl.

Saturday evening was cold but pleasant in Green Bay, with a full moon rising as we went to dinner and an early-to-bed evening. We awakened Sunday morning to find sub-zero (and plummeting) temperatures, but no snow—too cold to snow. Unprepared for this, we quickly had to find a downtown store to supplement our game attire. As one would expect on a Sunday morning, all businesses were closed and locked, except for an Army-Navy store, where the owner was taking year-end inventory. After much teeth-chattering persuasion, he opened his store.

We bought all the warm clothing we could find to keep out the freezing temperatures, including large garbage-type bags. We cut holes in the bottom of these to pull over our heads, and used adhesive tape to secure them around our waist. W.L. Gore didn't invent Gore-Tex until 1969—so he was no help for this game.

At game time, temperatures were still dropping from a minus-10 degrees with a wind-chill factor (man, that wind in cold weather is brutal) estimated somewhere between 30 and 40 degrees below. As an alternate my assignment was to be on the Packers' sideline and keep track of downs and distance as well as fouls called and enforced—writing it all down wearing three pairs of mittens!

Players on the bench huddled near the heaters—quarterbacks and receivers with their hands, kickers with their feet and me with my back-side nearest the warmth. Green Bay head coach Vince Lombardi, a New York-born rugged Italian, stood stoutly on the sideline (away from the heaters) the entire game. Prior to the last play, Packers quarterback Bart Starr came to the sideline to confer with Coach Lombardi (subsequently described as "Starr over Kramer at right guard for the touchdown" by announcer Ray Scott). Lombardi's words to Starr, who recommended the play: "Well, run the damn thing and let's get the hell outta here, it's getting cold." Final score: Green Bay 21, Dallas, 17.

 Will you maintain focus and determination when faced with trying conditions?

After further review …

In baseball, a brushback pitch is usually a fastball, thrown high and inside, designed to intimidate the batter. Announcers often describe that pitch as "high and tight" or "chin music." The intent, of course, is to keep a hitter from "digging in" or crowding the plate and narrowing the strike zone.

The first pitch in Game 3 of the recent World Series is a case in point. New York Mets starter Noah Syndergaard—who routinely reaches 100 mph on the radar gun—threw his first pitch head-high and inside off the glove of catcher Travis d'Arnaud, sprawling Royals free-swinging leadoff batter Alcides Escobar and in effect declaring "Batters Beware!"

Segue to NASCAR. The powers that be in that sport "parked" Matt Kenseth with a two-race suspension. Kenseth, the 2003 Sprint Cup champion and two-time Daytona 500 winner, delivered stock car racing's equivalent of a "brushback." According to NASCAR, Kenseth "intentionally wrecked" competitor Joey Logano's car at Martinsville (Virginia) Speedway on Nov. 1. Kenseth appealed but lost; his suspension is throughout the remainder of 2015.

NASCAR, somewhat like MLB, has usually taken the "boys will be boys" approach to such incidents. Wait just a dang minute! Those stock cars are racing at 170 mph-plus and the driver's life is at stake. The same could be said for MLB, since fastballs are traveling at 95 to 100 mph near a batter's head. Some may say, "Well, c'mon, man, it is what it is!" But just wait till a death occurs, and then see how these sports change. BTW, it's not an "all boys" situation. either. Pioneer female race car driver Danica Patrick was fined $50,000 for ramming David Gilliland's car during a yellow flag (a caution period) in that same Martinsville race.

It's about retaliation! Earlier this year at Kansas Speedway, Logano had caused a dramatic spinout on Kenseth's car as he was leading with four laps to go. And earlier in Martinsville, Gilliland had sent Patrick into the wall at Turn 3. Thus, the retaliation. In MLB it's practically an unwritten rule: you plunk one of our guys, we're going after one of yours. This is not healthy for the players, or the sport itself. And the eye-for-an-eye attitude of the pros trickles down through college and high school ranks, all the way down to youth little leagues. NASCAR officials have been criticized for their inconsistent enforcement of hazy rules. Maybe recent events are a wake-up call!

 Will you support a closer look at these practices that endanger the lives of others?

After further review …

Some may have heard Zach Johnson say in his press conference following his victory in the British Open at St. Andrews in July when he referred to Jordan Spieth: "He is a phenomenal golfer, but he is a much better person."

Here's a story that not a lot of people outside eastern Iowa know that tells you a lot about both men.

Johnson conducts a charity golf event every summer on the Monday before the John Deere tournament in the Quad Cities. He holds the event at Elmcrest Country Club in Cedar Rapids, where he learned to play golf and where his parents are still members. He invites a dozen professionals and a bunch of former athletes and coaches who are well-known Iowans. Any player can donate money to participate in a draft to pick the pro or celebrity with whom they then can play. There is also a silent auction on Sunday night during the pre-tournament banquet. At the end, he writes a check to match all of the money generated by the auctions and the draft.

Johnson's foundation distributes the money to public and private elementary and middle schools in the Cedar Rapids metro area. He also has donated a lot of money to various charities that were involved in relief and recovery efforts still occurring since the 2008 flood. When you hear Johnson say in his press conferences that golf creates opportunities, he is not talking about opportunities for him to make money—he is talking about opportunities to give money. He has been beyond generous and has never forgotten where he got his start.

But the real story here is about Spieth, who Johnson invited to play in this 2014 event; Spieth accepted, did play and further said he would return for the 2015 event. Now in 2015 Spieth wins the Masters and the U.S. Open, and competed at St. Andrews in The Open on a course he had never played nor ever seen. Spieth committed to Johnson that he would play in this year's Deere tournament. Spieth not only played in Quad Cities, but won spectacularly!

Here's what Johnson said: "Maybe it's just me, but the notion of that 21-year-old young man from Texas who is trying to win the third of three majors in a row had kept his commitment to play in this charity golf tournament just nine days before that Open is pretty remarkable."

 Will you keep the commitments you make—every time?

After further review …

Blame, blame, blame; it's one of our most renewable resources.

But no, this is not about the federal government—unless you want it to be. This column is about stepping-up to be responsible for your actions. Let me tell you a story.

During the NFL career of Dallas Cowboys quarterback Roger Staubach (1969-1979), I was privileged to officiate many of his games. The Cowboys and Philadelphia Eagles led by, respectively, the legendary Tom Landry and Ed Khayat, had what could be mildly described as a vicious rivalry.

Late in one game at Texas stadium, the 'Boys were leading the Eagles 38-0 when Staubach scrambled to his left to avoid a tackler, but tripped. (Sometimes those yard lines jump up at you.) I trailed Staubach some five or six yards and saw that no defensive player had caused his fall; he was free to get up and continue.

Yet it appeared that clumsy number 12 was not trying to get up so I blew my whistle to consider him down. At precisely the same moment I noticed the ball bouncing away from him. That's called a "loose ball" and may be advanced by either team. Eagles free safety Bill Bradley scooped it up and did just that, running forty yards for an apparent touchdown. (Bradley was a University of Texas All-American and playing his first NFL game in his home state.)

When Khayat heard the whistle, which stopped play, he started screaming unprintable evaluations of my judgment. I was 15 or so yards from him and did what I was taught to do. I walked to the Eagles' sideline toward the irate coach and said, "Ed, I kicked it. I shouldn't have blown that whistle and you should have six points. But I can't allow it." Needless to say, I was embarrassed, yet had to fortify my nerves to continue officiating.

Years later Khayat and I were at an NFL alumni event and he very cordially said, "Jim, you remember that call in Dallas some years back?" I sheepishly responded, "Ed, I sure do." The coach then said, "When you admitted your error, you disarmed me. There was nothing else I could say, since I've made mistakes and so have my players."

Rudyard Kipling's "If," long a source of inspiration for me, addresses such miscues with the lines, "If you can trust yourself when all men doubt you, but make allowance for their doubting, too... you'll be a man, my son."

 Will you step up to your responsibilities and not blame others?

After further review …

Millions of college football fans watched the No.1-ranked Florida State University Seminoles compete with the second-ranked Auburn University Tigers for the Bowl Championship game on Jan. 6.

Whether in attendance at the Rose Bowl or watching on ESPN, fans were treated to one the best college football games of the 2013 season—almost.

The BCS, a creation of college football administrators, has run its course. Beginning with the 2014 season Division 1 colleges and universities will invoke a playoff system involving the top four ranked teams. But FSU and Auburn need to be applauded for wrapping-up the BCS with a great game—almost.

Here's my take on "almost." FSU was trailing 21-13 in the fourth quarter when FSU defensive back P.J. Williams intercepted Auburn quarterback Nick Marshall's pass.

FSU quarterback Jameis Winston (the 2013 Heisman Trophy winner) completed a pass to Chad Abram, who hurdled an Auburn tackler and scored a touchdown to narrow the gap to 21-19.

Surely with FSU struggling to keep the score level, it would go for the two-point conversion ("try-for-point" as it is officially termed). The usual place kick for a single point wouldn't do it.

Then the unthinkable happened 1—here's where the "almost" comes in. Just after Abram scored, an FSU player was flagged by an official for taunting. Taunting, by definition, is an abusive act or verbal expression directed at an opponent. The trash-talking in this particular infraction is a 15-yard penalty, meaning that FSU's try-for-point would be attempted from the Auburn 17. Feeling that 17 yards was too much of a gamble for a run or pass, FSU coach Jimbo Fisher opted to go for the point-after kick, leaving the score 21-20 in favor of Auburn.

What was that FSU player thinking? Athletes at every level of every game must remember that sportsmanship is your responsibility! No player or T*E*A*M wants an opponent to rub their face in the dirt with trash talk. A sporting contest is anything but sporting if it's not played in an atmosphere of respect.

The FSU and Auburn teams gave their best effort in that BCS game (which FSU went on to win in dramatic fashion) and every player on both teams could walk away with pride in his effort—except one.

Will you treat your opponent with the same respect you expect him to show you?

After further review …

If you doubt the influence that pros have on younger players in college and high school, perhaps watching the NCAA's March Madness will give you a realistic perspective. Flopping abounds throughout basketball. By definition flopping is "an intentional fall by a player after little or no contact by an opposing player in order to draw a personal foul call by a game official."

The NBA added a rule in 1997 to cut down on this farcical act. Effectively ignored by both players and officials, the NBA had to begin fining guilty players in 2012 for this ludicrous maneuver. NCAA rule 10, 6f (and a similar National Federation of State High Schools rule) calls for a technical foul, but is seldom called.

In the NCAA championship basketball game being played tonight, flopping will be there for all to see. The charging/blocking foul in today's basketball game is the most difficult call for an official. With so much of the game now being played above the rim because of the size and strength of today's players, the drive to the basket is more prominent than ever. The debate continues, some players insisting that flopping has its tactical place, while many basketball purists say it makes a mockery of the game.

However, these TUNNEYSIDE columns are designed to transform issues from the world of sports into positive messages for everyday living. You might say, "Well, I don't play basketball, so I don't flop." Really? Did you ever intentionally not do your best? Did you ever try to trick others into believing it was someone else's fault and not yours? Flopping by simple definition is a failure to do your job. In basketball or any other sport flopping (in hockey it's called "diving") is a deliberate deception with the attempt to manipulate the official's judgment.

As a student, or as a businessperson, that tactic is dishonest and a failure to accept your responsibility. We know from studies that when people practice poor behavior in one part of their lives, it often occurs in other aspects of what they do.

 Will you accept responsibility in whatever you do?

ABOUT JIM TUNNEY

Jim Tunney has had an exemplary career in sports. A former high school coach, teacher, principal, and district superintendent, he had a 40-year career in officiating football and basketball. Thirty-one of those years, he was "the face of NFL officiating," working a record twenty-nine post-season games including three Super Bowls (two back-to-back), ten NFC/AFC Championship games, six Pro Bowls, and twenty-five Monday Night games, when MNF was THE game of the week. He officiated some of the most memorable games in NFL history, including "The Ice Bowl," "The Kick," "The Snowball Game," "The Final Fumble," "The Fog Bowl," and "The Catch." His book *IMPARTIAL JUDGMENT: The "Dean of NFL Referees" Calls Pro Football as He Sees It* chronicles his NFL career. Seven times, he has been nominated for the NFL Hall of Fame.

As a professional speaker, he is past president of the National Speakers Association and a charter member of its most prestigious group—The CPAE Speakers Hall of Fame. Jim holds every professional designation of the NSA, including the Philanthropist of the Year and the Cavett—the Oscar of professional speaking.

Dr. Tunney (he received a doctorate in education from the University of Southern California) continues to serve his community as a former headmaster and trustee of York School and former trustee of the Monterey Peninsula College. MPC honored him with its President's Award in 2009. Moreover, that same year he was awarded the Citizen of the Year by the Monterey Chamber of Commerce.

In 1993, he founded the Jim Tunney Youth Foundation to support local community programs that develop leadership, work skills, wellness, and self-esteem in youth. To date, the JTYF has made grants exceeding a quarter million dollars.

He has been inducted into the California Community College Football Hall of Fame and the Multi-Ethnic Sports Hall of Fame, as well as being the first administrator inducted into the Fairfax High School Hall of Fame.

As an author he has written and/or co-authored nine books: *Impartial Judgment; Chicken Soup for the Sports Fan's Soul; Super Bowl Sunday; Speaking Secrets of the Masters; Lessons in Leadership; Insights into Excellence; You Can Do It!; Build a Better You;* and, *It's the Will, Not the Skill.* He continues to write a weekly column for the *Monterey County Herald,* called "On the TUNNEYSIDE of Sports."